Roxane Christ

I am (not) a Hero, I am a Survivor

The Story of
Lou Van Coevorden

authorHOUSE™

1663 LIBERTY DRIVE, SUITE 200
BLOOMINGTON, INDIANA 47403
(800) 839-8640
WWW.AUTHORHOUSE.COM

First published by AuthorHouse 09/20/04

ISBN: 1-4184-9747-9 (sc)

Printed in the United States of America
Bloomington, Indiana

This book is printed on acid-free paper.

ACKNOWLEDGEMENTS

We hereby acknowledge the invaluable contribution of those institutions, organizations and universities who have made it possible for us to reproduce the photographs appearing in this book.

We wish to thank the following people,

Anthony E. Anderson
International Documents Librarian
Von KleinSmid Library
University of Southern California

Maren L. Read
Photo Research Coordinator, Photo Archives
United States Holocaust Memorial Museum

Paul Eugen Camp
University of South Florida Library

Holly Reed
United States National Archives

And the following organizations,
KZ Gedenkstaette Dachau
Nederlands Institut voor Oorlogsdocumentatie
The Simon Wiesenthal Center Library & Archives

For their time and efforts

We must be ruthless...Only thus shall we purge our people of their softness...and their degenerate delight in beer-swelling...I don't want the concentration camps transformed into penitentiaries. Terror is the most effective political instrument...It is my duty to make use of every means of training the German people to cruelty, and to prepare them for war...There must be no weakness or tenderness.

Adolf Hitler

EDITORIAL

This book is the recital of three years in a man's life. It is not a common story, yet it is a story of horrors known to men the world over. It doesn't depict atrocities of World War II in the normal course of one's history books. Lou Van Coevorden was only a boy when he embarked on his voyage through hell. But his determination to avenge his suffering and the death of his family is detailed day after day throughout his journey.

There are three factors in this book which should be taken into consideration by the reader. Firstly, not all Jews are equal – the rich ones had the opportunity to survive because they chose to use their wealth to save their lives. Secondly, Jews are not equal inasmuch as whether they are issued from different backgrounds, solidarity is not found amongst them. And finally, when it comes to avenge their suffering, they will do it with only accepting and resenting the pain of their vengeful acts.

The participation of the Allied Forces in the Jewish revenge is blatant throughout the last episodes of the

Second World War. What is also evident however, is that there are no animosity, no remorse, no wanting of rewards for heroism on the part of Lou Van Coevorden. He is now one of the last survivors of the concentration camps in Germany and when he saw the downfall of Auschwitz his glee couldn't be contained but neither could it be expressed. Lou Van Coevorden was spent, yet at the age of twenty one he was to fight for his life many times over even though the Second World War had ended. After living in hell he couldn't return to life – he needed to deny himself the vision of the faces that haunted him at every turn; the faces of those who had not been able to survive.

As for me, I am only a writer who saw in Lou Van Coevorden the opportunity to tell the story of some of my family – the ones who didn't make it; those whom I will never meet, those who have disappeared because they were of another race.

I wish for this book to be an inspiration for future generations and a guiding thought for those who would be led by leaders thirsty for power and lusting for the sadistic enthroning of their imaginary strength.

Roxane P.A. Christ
May, 2004

PREFACE

When I meet people and tell them I survived the Holocaust, I am told how lucky I am to be alive, instead of their turning it around to tell me how they are the lucky ones because they were spared all that suffering. Why is it, for them, a normal thing and for me, luck is to be alive?

How lucky can you be? When you find on your return you have lost everyone around you. An orphan receives sympathy because he lost his parents, and he is never told that he should be lucky to be alive. So where lays my luck? Am I lucky because I lost all my friends and family?

Since 1945, I have been trying to find my luck back. But with all the misery cast upon me by the Nazis, luck will never be complete anymore. In our case, it is every silver lining that has a cloud; instead of the other way around.

Every movie cast about the terrible time has a happy ending. Not so in real life. But, instead of dwelling on the fact, I have decided to write my memoirs about my camp experience and the non-existence of any guidance back into normal life.

CHAPTER I
Family Life
Episodes of Fortune and Misfortune

It all started on a wintry day in 1924 when I was born. My parents lived in Amsterdam at the time, in a neighborhood that became a Nazi ghetto in 1941. As a newborn baby, you are not aware of the things going on around you. Your parents protect you from all kinds of trouble. And to be born into a Jewish family gives you an edge; the 'Jiddische Mama'! She is the Head of the Family. She seldom punishes you. This is left to Daddy, when he comes home from work. But she will tell you all day long, "Wait 'til Daddy comes home. He will give you a spanking you'll never forget." And when he comes home she asks him to take care of that terrible son of his. But when he lifts his hand to spank you, she is the one who screams, "Are you crazy to hit my kid?"

It is not hard to please them either. All kids that are born into a Jewish family are geniuses in their parents' eyes. But when you are naughty or bad, you lose one parent. Then you become *his* son! When you do something real nice or accomplish something they did not expect, all of a sudden, you become *her* son. Only to the outside world you are *their* son no matter what happens.

My parents were very pleased with me; I would be able to preserve the family name. This used to be very important, but only to one side of the family. And as it happened to me, I was to carry the Van Coevorden name; which was the poor side of the family. To the other side you were just *another* grandchild.

I was born in a neighborhood where everybody was poor, and so were we. We lived across from the Welfare Department. And our income was so low that we were entitled to food stamps; when everyone else ate butter we ate margarine. I was the only Jewish boy attending a Protestant nursery school, and I prayed like everybody else to God, thanking him for my daily meal. I did not realize I was different from the other kids because I was Jewish. Kids don't discriminate; not until they are taught by adults to do so later in life.

The family bonds were tight. Parents watched over their children day and night. Babysitters were out of the question. When once in a while there was some extra money to see a show, the babies were wrapped tightly in blankets and taken along to the show.

When I was about four years old, we moved to a new place. It was a more comfortable house, and we went off the welfare rolls. My father found a job as a waiter, and my mother worked at home as a seamstress. This neighborhood was a Jewish neighborhood. It meant that you had to conform to what, to me, were *new customs*. Even though a few people were Orthodox, everybody kept strictly to the Jewish holidays. On those occasions, our Christian friends had to attend school while we were off for a religious holiday. Oh, did they want to be Jewish too!

Our new neighborhood was more like a clan. If somebody was in financial trouble, word would spread like wildfire and food was supplied to anybody who needed it. Refrigerators were non-existent, so leftovers were kept in a chicken wire cage outside the window. On Friday chicken soup was made to last the weekend. Thus, anyone who was too proud to concede their poverty put an empty tureen in the outside cage. Then a neighbor, without fail, would bring soup, because the 'chicken man' had told him that you hadn't bought anything from him that week.

Sundays were special because of our market where merchants sold their wares in a way rarely found in other parts of the world. Some of them were real entertainers, and we had a ball watching them sell their goods. They recommended the purchase of their products with such skills that many people who had come only to watch the show became customers against their will. The rest of the week, we took

3

possession of the streets to play soccer. Neighborhood teams were formed, without any parental help. And many of those kids turned into star soccer players just by learning from each other. Scouts for soccer clubs went around looking for talent for their clubs. That is how I was selected, at the age of ten, to play in a *real club*. A.E.D. was the name of the club. Somebody from the club picked me off the street and bought me a complete outfit, in a sport's shop. The following Sunday, I played a practice game against Ajax Juniors as center forward. I scored two goals and we won the game. During the game, a heavy set man was watching us from behind one of the goals. After the game I was introduced to him. He was the *Big Banana* of the club – in more than one way; not only because he, more or less, owned the club, but he also owned a banana plant. This man, whom I met for the first time in my young life turned out to be my grandfather.

The reason I did not meet this man before that day was due to my mother's reluctance to adhere to the family tradition whereby the man she had to marry had to be chosen by her parents. She had stubbornly and rightfully married the man she loved and was banned from the rich part of the family. My sister and I did not even know about the *other side* of the family; to us they did not exist.

The banana plant was a place where they ripened the fruits and prepared them for distribution across the Netherlands. And now that I had found out about my grandfather's banana plant; which was only a block away from the school I attended, I took advantage of my new found Granddaddy and went to see him

4

on a daily basis and got a banana for lunch. When my cousin, Jettie, discovered how easy it was to get a banana by just saying 'hello' to Granddaddy, she too made this, a daily habit. This would eventually lead to disaster for one of her girlfriends.

On that occasion Jettie took her girlfriend along. Sonja was not allowed to enter the plant; so she waited by the front door. When Jettie returned, Sonja was not there anymore. We did not worry about it since we were already kind of late for school; we thought she might have gotten tired of waiting and went to school without our knowledge. Jettie and I made it just in time to beat the school bell. But when we entered the classroom, we discovered that Sonja wasn't there. 'Maybe she went home sick,' we thought. Later in the evening, when we were contacted by Sonja's mother, who inquired whether we knew anything about Sonja's whereabouts, we began to worry. The police was informed and an investigation started. The only clue they had was that we left her at the front door of the banana plant. My grandfather was called to the police station for questioning, but was released within a few hours. Two days went by without any result. Hence, a famous forensic specialist by the name of Malowich was called in. After walking around for awhile blindfolded; a lot of commotion surrounding his strange search due to the hundreds of spectators watching him, he deduced that the body should be found in a banana container in the attic of the plant. We had a nice view of what was going on from across the street where we lived. At about 11:00pm, my grandfather was asked to come down and open up the plant. And, indeed, the little body was found, spread eagle in a banana container. The murderer was somebody who had helped continuously for two days with the investigation. The man was arrested at once.

The significance of the fact and the irony of it perhaps, is that the murderer, who was sentenced to twenty years imprisonment, survived the war in jail which saved him from death in a concentration camp. He was one of our own, known as a quiet, gentle person.

The community was outraged and astonished. Being investigated like a criminal was quite a shock to my grandfather. And even when it was all over, we were banned from the plant. Therefore, the only way, to keep the contact going between my grandfather and me, was to visit him at home. Up until then I had not met my grandmother – at least I thought I hadn't; but when I met her at her home in a plush part of town, I realized that I had met her before then. The first time was in a kind of an embarrassing situation, which I will never forget.

I was playing outside one day, when a lady walked up to me and asked me to follow her into a shoe store. There, she told the clerk that she wanted to buy a pair of shoes for a poor boy. I was fitted with a pair of new shoes and went home and told my mother a lady had bought me a pair of shoes. When I described to my mother what the lady, who had bought me the shoes, looked like, she ordered me to return the shoes at once. I was too proud of my new shoes to give in, so I called on my father to help me convince my mother to let me keep them but didn't succeed. Up 'til now I cannot understand how a grandparent could do such a thing to a grandchild!

I guess the establishment of the credit card era came into existence via a system which, we, poor people, had to go by. It happened very often that at the end of the month people ran out of money. And when food was needed, it was not uncommon to send the kids to the store to buy food on credit. We kids did not know any better. All we had to do was to tell the grocer to write it down (which meant charge it to our account), and our little arms were filled with whatever we needed.

Soon, I found out that candy was also available by just saying, 'charge it!' I didn't know that I was doing anything wrong, and every day, I got my candies by just saying, 'charge it'. Everything went fine until, at the end of the month, my mother was presented with the bill... Boy was she mad! That night my father *really* convinced me, via a spanking, never to do it again.

The next few years were uneventful until all of a sudden disaster struck the rich part of the family. The banana business went from bad to worse. Bad management and embezzlement got the business into trouble; so much money had been embezzled actually that it had been impossible to save the company from bankruptcy.

The effect on my grandfather was incredible – a whole lifetime of work in shambles. In a very short time, he ended up in a 'nut house'. I could not believe the change that occurred in my grandfather in such a short time. This brought my parents finally back into the clan. I don't know how it affected my grandmother, but she did not change her lifestyle a bit.

Once in a while I went to visit my grandfather. Why? I don't know why. He was absolutely not aware of me and did not speak one coherent word. All he did was to bang his head against the wall and utter some words nobody understood. He shrank from a giant of a man into a man with whom nobody wanted to associate. How cruel to a man so gentle. All of the people who 'loved' him so much when he was wealthy let him down after his luck left him.

CHAPTER II

Adolescence

The Realization of Character

In Germany, a man named Hitler was on the rise to leave his mark by suppressing all minorities, especially Jews. Pictures and articles appeared in the Dutch newspapers showing riots and beatings imposed on innocent people, but even though we sympathized with the poor victims, it was far from our bed and did not concern us.

'We were different; this could never happen in our country. Our people would not stand for it.' And when we read about concentration camps, it had no meaning to us, and even now, when I talk about my experience to other people, they look at me like I am somebody from another planet. Nobody can comprehend the damage done – unless you were there...

My growing up in a family where discipline was an everyday law helped me greatly in my struggle for life during my concentration camp days. My father was very tough, and I got my punishment whenever he felt I went out of hand. Sometimes I did not deserve to be spanked, but I got beaten anyway. His typical answer to this situation was: "If you did not do it now, consider this beating to be in advance for the next time I do not catch you in the act". Those occasional beatings hardened me and made me promise myself that nobody was ever going to get down on me without me getting revenge.

It all happened one evening when my father wrongfully accused me of something I had not done; when he closed in on me, I told him that if he beat me now he would have a fight on his hands. Suddenly, he backed off – not because he was afraid, but, I think, he saw my coming of age. After this incident the bond between my father and me became closer than ever before, and he became a real friend for me.

The family decided to move to another location. This would benefit us, because houses were plentiful and there were vacancies everywhere; landlords offered their apartments with one-month free rent to fill their properties. So, we moved to another neighborhood again.

Luckily, it was not too far off, and I could keep my old friends. It was there that I joined the Labor Youth Organization, and soon our house became a 'youth center', but not for long. A few months later it was moving time again.

The new address would become my parents' last destination. The moving was done by my father and me to save money. All day long we went back and forth, loading everything in the cart, which we pushed by hand. At around 5:00pm we called it a day. There was only the stuff from the Youth Organization left at the house to be transferred the next day.

The house was already occupied by the new tenant, when we returned and asked permission to retrieve the rest of our belongings. The man told us, in no uncertain terms that the house and everything in it was now *his*. The argument heated up, and all of a sudden, he lunged at my father. In a reflex, I hit him on the chin; he went down cold, and, before he came to, we were gone. The first lesson I learned from my father was never to stand with my back turned, in a stairwell, in the middle of a fight.

The whole family was proud of my action. They acted like I save my father's life; even though he was twice as strong and wiser too. I was so elated by all the praise that I wanted to go back the next day, but my father kept me from doing so. I don't know what happened to the equipment that had been left behind, but I never saw any of it again.

Our new address was a very nice place to live. My sister and I had our own room – for the first time.

I entered College when my sister Jetty went to elementary school. She was fifteen years old when she was taken to a concentration camp together with my mother and, they both died of typhus in Sweden in 1945.

Even though I wanted to work as soon as possible to help support our family, the decision was made that I should finish my education first. But even before my final examination I had found myself a job as an apprentice in a pastry shop.

My parents did not know I had a job, but they did not object when they found out about it. It had always been my wish to be a pastry worker so that I could eat as much as I could. My wages were only one dollar a week, but I ate so much whipped cream; that I felt if I continued doing this, sooner or later I would become a little doughboy myself.

Seeing my predicament my mother suggested that I apply for a job as an apprentice cloth presser at Hollandia Kattenburg. I was hired at a much better salary, and I really loved every minute I worked there.

Sunday was my soccer day, and our team was doing very well. The decisive game for the league championship was coming up the following Sunday – an event, I did not want to miss.

But as it happens, I did something against my father's will during the week before the game. A Beating was out of the question; the new punishment came in the form of grounding. I was confined to my room and forbidden to play in Sunday's game. My shoes were taken away, and the situation looked hopeless.

The team counted on me, and I did not want to let them down. My only escape route was through a roof-top window inside my own room – a kind of skylight. It took me a while to pry the window open; then I grabbed the rim of the window and lifted myself onto the roof. From there it was only ten feet down to the school grounds behind us. The hardest job was yet ahead of me. In order to get into the next street, I had to climb the drainage pipe to the roof of the school building. It was a daring task. If the rain drainage pipe did not hold, I would be in real trouble. Very carefully, I started to climb, stopping once in a while to make sure the pipe would hold. Lucky for me, the pipe held and soon I found myself on top of the three-story school building. Sliding down was a cinch and after a short rest – I did. I landed in the next street without any trouble. I ran barefoot in order to make it in time for the game. The game was just about to start, and when my friends discovered what I did, they went wild. This team was a real team – if anyone of us had been missing, the chance of winning would not have been as good.

Somebody got me an outfit in a hurry, and we were ready to go… I did not worry about the consequences of my escape. I played totally free of concern and scored the only and winning goal during the first half of the game. At half time I saw a familiar figure – for the first and last time ever, my father, who hated soccer, was there. He was a good sport and let me play the second half without any interference. Right after the game he took me home. I could not join the party. I knew there would be more punishment for my escape, but I did not worry. The times of beatings were gone, and I did not care what kind of punishment was in store as long as we became champions. We made it, and I really do not remember what sanction I got in the end. Even at Hollandia, word went around that we had won the championship. And all of a sudden my popularity was on the rise.

Up until that time, I had never had anything to do with girls. I devoted all my free time to soccer and had no time for other activities. Now that the season was over however, I had time on my hands. I was sixteen, young and handsome, but I was shy. One girl, Mijntje, drew my attention when she brought me all kinds of candies during breaks. I got very fond of her, and she became my first girlfriend. Not for long however. When she told me that she had a boyfriend before me, who would commit suicide if she didn't go back to him, I advised her to return to him.

At my age, it was customary to have a girlfriend, and, when Anny asked me to become her boyfriend I accepted her proposal. Anny was a woman of the world, and I was a greenhorn as far as women were concerned. I don't think she understood why I showed so little interest in her. For me, a girl was just a nice companion 'to have around and to go places with' – when there was nothing else to do. And maybe it was this innocence or ignorance that attracted her to me. Anny had never met my parents, but on her first visit to our house, when I was ill with an ulcer, she was sized up by my father and mother. The impression she made was not very good. When we were left alone in the room she made advances and even kissed me. Then she put herself on top of me, fully dressed. All I could think of was that I wished she would stop. When I did not respond to her advances she decided it was time to leave. About a week later, I received a letter from her suggesting we break-up our relationship, because it would not work out. She also wrote that she was a prostitute who went to bed with anybody who would pay for her services. I felt sorry for her and made up my mind to help her get out of the business. I was so naïve to write to her telling her not to worry and that I would take care of her problem. Carefully, I put her letter under my mattress hoping that my parents would not find it. The next day they confronted me, letter in hand. I was questioned about what I was going to do about this girl. Their lecture made me more confident that I was the only one who could save her... However, I did not know how. But the problem would solve itself through circumstances beyond anyone's control.

The Germans enter Amsterdam...
(May 1940)

CHAPTER III
Coming of Age

Entering Manhood –
Personally and Politically

May 1940, the Germans invade Holland. As a sixteen-year-old boy, the invasion of your country is something you cannot understand, the meaning of which you cannot grasp. It is like a game when it starts. And you are not involved, but when it lasts too long and the invader behaves like the Germans did, it becomes a nightmare.

Holland was absolutely not prepared for war. They thought if they declared themselves 'neutral', such as they did in World War I, they would be safe. But to be effectively 'neutral' you need a mutual agreement, and Germany was not receptive to our declaration of neutrality. Armed with outdated equipment; we were an easy target. All we could do was to inundate a great deal of our country to slow them down. (A vast majority of Holland is located *below* sea level, therefore 'flooding' parts of our country didn't present that much of a problem.) The Germans, for their part however, equipped with modern weaponry, found no match in us. It took them only four days to conquer our country. All we could do now was to wait and see what the future would hold.

Everybody believed this war would be a short one. It would be over in six months, people said. The occupation did not change anything in our every day routine during the first few months; everything was quiet and peaceful. And if it were not for the visible presence of Germans in uniforms walking down the streets, you would not even have noticed that the country was at war. We did not associate with *them* and they left *us* alone. The effect the war had on our daily life was absolutely nil. But that would soon change.

Slowly but decisively, it began. First it was the production changes in the factories; at Hollandia we switched from making raincoats to making military uniforms. But who cares? Pressing one seam or another – it was all the same.

The first indication that things were going to change came when the Dutch Nazis acted as if they were 'in charge'; such as a political party would. Originally they were hardly able to sustain themselves, but, with a powerful friend backing them now, they became bold and aggressive. During the invasion they were so scared the Germans would not succeed that they stayed out of sight as much as possible.

Their leader, a man by the name of Anton Mussert, made himself the laughing stock of Holland by hiding in a haystack on a farm until the war was over and until he was no longer in fear for his life.

Before the war we had never seen a Nazi uniform in our Jewish neighborhood. But with Germany' support, the Dutch Nazis felt strong enough now to provoke us by marching through the streets of our neighborhood in uniform.

When that did not bring any satisfactory result, they tried insulting us publicly – and that too, was to no avail. Only when they became violent by smashing windows and molesting people that we realized time had come to resist.

We formed a defense league. It was organized so that we, kids who roamed the streets anyhow, would notify the adults in case of looming trouble. And, when they came down Amstel Street, one day, with the intention of again smashing windows and attacking people, we were prepared for them.

When they approached Waterloo square, our boys were there to meet them head on. We fought them off with bats and bricks. One of their men, by the name of Koot, made the fatal mistake of underestimating our will to resist. He decided to take a car and try running us down. He did not get far. An ax was thrown through the windshield forcing him to stop. He was pulled out of the car and became the first victim of our 'defense force'.

Waterloo Square Market

Retaliation from the German camp was soon to be felt however. Fifteen Jewish men were picked off the street at random the next day by the SS forces and sent to one of the worst concentration camps, Mauthausen.

Another provocation, in the Dutch Nazis' mind, was Koot's funeral being routed through our neighborhood. All of us watched the parade go by from our 'window seats' with glee.

And when people asked about our resistance – why we did not resist? All I can say is that resistance was there. The only thing was that it was not organized – but individually managed, if you like. Violent resistance was out of the question for the moment; this would be crushed in no time and would result in more people being picked up. So, we became very inventive in our way of 'resisting the invader'.

A case in point is how we celebrated our royal family's birthday. Our prince was known to wear a white carnation everywhere he went. So, out of the blue, everybody wore a white carnation on his birthday. To the Germans this did not mean anything at all. But to the Dutch Nazis this was an insult of the first magnitude. It had the same effect as a red flag has on a bull. People were stopped and carnations torn off their lapels. When this became known, we countered the action by hiding razor blades in our carnations – which resulted in bloody surprises without reprisal. We had made our point. The Dutch Nazis in time realized that they could not take effective action against us without the support of their German friends.

The first action taken by the Germans (without the Dutch Nazis' assistance) was against a German Jew who owned a flourishing ice cream parlor in Rynstreet, an affluent Jewish neighborhood in Amsterdam. They decided to put a halt to his business under the pretext that it was the headquarters of an underground-organized gang. When they arrived at the place, the owner was prepared for them. In force, they smashed the front door and all of the windows and entered the parlor. But at the same moment – as they entered the premises, they were sprayed with acid. A few of them were blinded and the owner, who fought like a lion, did not survive the ordeal. He was killed at his place of work but had disfigured some enemies for life. This incident resulted in orders from SS Headquarters to arrest 400 Jews between the ages of twenty and thirty-five to be sent to concentration camps in Germany.

SS troops roamed the city picking up people at random. This was something to which we had to respond; But how? With force would be counter-productive because it would give the Germans additional reasons to continue their 'razias'. (Since the Germans needed more and more able-bodied men to go to work in their enterprises, factories, or labor camps –their own people being sent to the front by the thousands, any pretext was good to pick-up more men.)

Help came in a way we did not expect. Handbills were handed out, asking everybody to strike "in support of our Jewish friends and against German brutality". Everybody felt insecure, the strike took off slowly, but around noon on that day, we found ourselves in the throws of a complete general strike. Street-cars were not running; factories closed up. Everyone took to the streets in peaceful demonstrations in support of our people. The strike lasted only one day, but the support we got from our fellow citizens was heart-warming.

The Germans accelerated theirs orders then. We were first prohibited from listening to foreign broadcasts – under the penalty of death! So we hid our radios in our closets, at BBC news time there was always someone missing from every family. The broadcasts kept us up-to-date with the development in the war effort, which in turn helped our resistance efforts greatly.

But all of these orders from the Germans were just minor annoyances – the beginning of things to come. It would be worse than anyone could ever imagine. German citizens were not allowed to serve Jewish families any more. And, my grandmother lost her German maid. And it did not hurt us when orders came down saying that government agencies were not permitted to hire Jewish people for employment. However, it was a different story when those already employed were dismissed without compensation – on German orders. No benefits were to be allocated either, which put those people in an impossible position. An action was taken by government employees to offer 1% of their salary to compensate those who had lost their job. This show of solidarity was the greatest gesture they could make to boost our morale.

Then, in order to separate the Jewish community from the rest of the population, restrictions were put upon us in the form of new orders. Curfew was imposed; nobody was allowed outdoors between 8:00pm and 6:00am. This order affected people of all ages.

As a consequence, we had to change our lifestyle completely. Family life became closer than ever as a result. Even though we were not allowed outdoors, there were other ways to get together. All houses were connected by fire escape routes, so, after 8:00pm these routes suffered from 'traffic congestion' created by people visiting each other to play cards or just to lift their spirits sitting around and talking. Actually, hanging out of the windows talking to each other became the neighborhood's favorite pastime. We even got a closer relationship with our non-Jewish neighbors; and we relied on them totally for information about upcoming 'razias'. Police officers would inform them of the time and place for the next scheduled razia; they in turn, would inform us so we could avoid getting caught.

One such man was Uncle Jan – our neighborhood barkeeper. He had his own bar at the corner of our street. It was a place where we, as teenagers, hung out to play billiards. He was about seventy years old. Everybody loved him. He was a kind of second father to all of us. We knew we were safe at his place. Once in a while, when there was a surprise razia, he would shield us with his own body. He would put himself in the doorway and nobody would have dared testing Uncle Jan's authority. Even the Germans respected him. And while he was delaying them, his daughter would lead us to safety. This was made possible because of the advance warning system and our artistic way of dodging the enemy.

The Germans were forced to look for other ways to get their daily quota of Jews. In many instances it was very hard to distinguish between Jews and non-Jews. Therefore, we were ordered to register and to get identification cards. This registration was put in place for us as well as for gentiles. The only difference was that our cards would show a big "J", identifying us as Jews. Since no one in his right mind would register as Jew with the German authorities, our religious leaders were drafted to put the enrolment in place. They did such an effective job of it that only very few of us did not register.

Our trust in our leaders would cost us dearly. Every Jew was marked now and ripe and ready to be picked up at will. The ultimate goal was to exterminate all Jews but in the first instance the selection was not as random as it may have appeared. Since Jewish blood is transmitted by the mother of a family, Jewish women of all ages were the first targets to be transported to the gas-chambers. In a family where the mother was Jewish, she and her children would be sentenced to death – leaving the Christian father to mourn their passing. And, when the father was the Jewish member of a mixed family – he would be sent to concentration camp. This imposed segregation and disposition of a family unit would hit everyone (Christians and Jews alike) very hard.

Every Friday, new orders were issued to spoil our weekends. The only thing of which we were not sure was what their next ploy would be and how we could counter their orders. One of these orders affected everyone living in Amsterdam (and every person living in Holland, I am sure). We were told that we had to bring our bicycles to a designated place in the city... That order was, if not ridiculous, extremely inconvenient for most people. In Holland the vehicle of choice to make your way easily through the city is the bicycle. Therefore, by ordering us to hand those over, the Germans were making life more difficult for everyone, once again. And if you didn't follow that order, and a German officer would catch you riding a bike in the street, it would be confiscated on the spot.

One Thursday, members of my club informed me that I had been selected to play in the top soccer team. I could not believe it. People I looked up to and idolized were all of a sudden going to be 'team mates'. The excitement was overwhelming.

But, I was struck with disbelief when I read in the Friday night paper (the night we usually got the 'bad orders') that we, as Jews, were banned from attending movie theaters and from attending or participating in sports events. That meant I could not *participate* in the soccer game! How could they do such a thing *to me* – nobody was going to stop me. So, on Sunday I went to the playing field. I took my dog with me; I got it from the pound a few weeks earlier and as we walked onto the field, I could not believe my eyes. All we encountered was deadly silence. Our opponent wasn't even there. For the first time I felt the full extent of German power. I was powerless. I felt sick to my stomach. Then I realized that there would not be any soccer for me as long as we were under German occupation. How would I fill my weekends now?

I was still standing in the middle of the field, bewildered when suddenly my dog got loose and jumped me! I have no idea why he attacked me, but he did. He got on top of me and out of sheer rage and frustration I chocked him until he passed out... I left him where he was and walked home. I was despondent and inwardly crying tears of anger.

Then almost overnight neighborhood youth groups were formed. Boys and girls hung around on street corners; our headquarters was a little candy store. We organized parties where we danced and listened to music. On those occasions we were forced to stay overnight because of the imposed curfew.

It was at one such party that I met a sweet little girl; Henny Hakker was her name. I liked her a lot, and we were just good friends. I was too shy to ask her out on a date, and even less daring to ask her to be my girlfriend. The only reason we got together in the first place was that everyone else was engaged and we were the only couple left over. I suppressed my feeling about her, and our relationship was just a convenient friendship until one of us would express his feelings or would find someone else. I still feel guilty for not having talked to her when it was possible. It might have saved her life.

When 'our youth clan' gathered one day, my friend, Gerrie, was missing. Nobody knew anything of his whereabouts – not even his girlfriend, my cousin Jettie. We went to Gerrie's house, but nobody answered the doorbell or opened the door. There had not been a razia lately; the neighbors did not see them leave. I was all very mysterious. Something was wrong. A feeling of insecurity invaded everyone – somehow it broke the cohesion of the clan. Later, after the war, I learned that they were the first people who went underground, and the whole family survived the war.

Very often the question is asked: "Why didn't everyone go underground?" In reply I shake my head at the ignorance shown by the person asking such a question. There was no organized underground escape route yet; and even if there had been an organized effort, there would have been no way to hide 140,000 thousand people whenever the Germans found a better way to fill their quota of Jews.

27

They prohibited Jews from moving without their permission. The Jewish section of town was now enclosed with barbwire, and bridges were withdrawn at night. They had total control over us. We were trapped. But because they did not order the non-Jews out of the created ghettos, we had the opportunity to call on our non-Jewish friends when hiding was necessary.

We were trapped in our own neighborhood

During the day we could move freely to go to our place of work outside the ghetto. Jewish businesses had to be registered. They were to be confiscated at a later date. All non-Jewish stores were ordered to put a sign in the window telling all Jews that they were not welcome or allowed entry into these stores. Stiff penalty would be imposed on any non-Jews selling their wares to Jews. Our stores became dependent on the Germans for supplies. In the early stages of the occupation, when there was plenty of food, the supplies were adequate, but when food and daily necessities became scarce, we were the first to suffer. We were not allowed to sell our businesses. In many cases the Germans confiscated stores and just handed them to Nazi sympathizers whom they simply installed on the premises without providing any form of compensation to the evicted and dispossessed owner. We counter-acted this order by giving the business to our non-Jewish friends. Selling was out of the question. It had to be an outright *gift*. In such cases we still kept control over our property. Agreements were ratified whereby the business would be returned to us if any of us should return. The same procedure was followed with some of our babies. And even though many of the properties were returned to their rightful owners after the war, we would be facing big problems as far as placing babies were concerned. There were cases where people went to court and where sisters tried to get their younger siblings back to the fold. Often they were unable to do so because the judge found that since the natural parents had not returned, the step-parents were the appropriate parents now; they were better capable of taking care of the children than the related family.

Another injustice done to us – those kids were saved *for Christ* against their family's wishes. To put in another way, they were forcibly converted.

Now that the ghettos were created, it was easy to pick off Jews when needed. The German SS roamed the ghettos for kicks, playing cat and mouse with us. You never knew where they were or what they were up to

One day I got the fright of my life. When I went window shopping, I stopped in front of a pastry store where we bought our pastries when it was still permitted. Longingly I looked in the window and noticed the sign "No Jews Allowed." The sun was shining. I could see my reflection in the window. All of a sudden two SS gendarmes posted themselves next to me – one on each side. I told myself to keep calm. I had to make a decision. I could run, but that would make matters worse, so I took the bold step and entered the store. When I closed the door behind me, the gendarmes disappeared. I breathed a sigh of relief; I had made the right decision. Still, scared and tense I went home and released my tension by crying out loud.

Every day of freedom counted, but how long can somebody live under such restricted freedom? I guess in order to be saved from deportation; Misters Assher and Cohen decided to form the Jewish Council in view of establishing a link between the Jewish Community and the Germans.

They elected themselves as Head of the Council and were willingly accepted by the Germans. Now the Germans could make sure that their orders were carried out via the Jewish Council. The Council would put out the orders in a more digestible form to soften the blow.

One of the first orders was that everyone who had more than two Jewish grandparents, had to wear the Star of David, visible on his clothing. Even the size and the color of it were determined. Therefore, it was no longer necessary to check your identification. And even though I was (and I am) proud to be of Jewish descent, I decided not to be an easy target and to take a chance by not wearing the Star of David.

Another measure that was taken was the confiscation of our radios. We had just bought a new radio when this order came into effect – and we were not about to hand it to the Germans. We traded ours for Uncle Jan's, who had an old radio, and handed the piece of junk to the Germans with great pleasure.

On January 28th, my parents and I were trapped in a razia. We were on our way to celebrate my grandfather's birthday. It was about 7:00pm when we were stopped by the SS. When we told them that we were on our way to a birthday party they let us continue without any further questions or without asking for identifications.

A little ways ahead, all around us, we saw men on their knees, their hands on their heads; in their eyes we could see their feelings. They were scared of the unknown. Military trucks appeared in the dark of night; they came our way. In a jerk I pulled my father into a nearby basement to weather the storm. Meanwhile, my mother and sister made their way to my grandparent's house. When it felt safe to come out, we went on a couple blocks and finally arrived at destination. Everything was quiet, as if nothing had happened. A lot of people must have wondered if their father or husband would come home that night. You never knew... We rang the doorbell in our special and familiar way. The door was opened and everyone was relieved to seeing us.

I think if people would have realized that eventually everybody's turn would come up to be deported it wouldn't have been so easy to divide us. But because every human being has self-preservation at heart, it was easy to divide the community by just putting us in 'classifications'. The importance of a person was decided according to his impact on the economy. Everybody had a number of 'importance', which you had to show when stopped. And if you were stopped they would let you go because could fill their daily quota easily with people who were not '*sperred*' – as it was called. And even though you felt sorry for the people who were arrested, you were glad not to be one of them and to be *sperred*. We figured if we could hold out for another six months we would be safe, because the war would be over by then...

Presenting your identification card on request

If one person was *sperred*, it protected the rest of the family. So it happened very often that a *sperred* person would marry an '*unsperred*' one with the intention to annul the marriage after the war was over. Thus, when my aunt asked me whether I was willing to marry Henny Hakker, the girl I liked so much, I was pleased to agree immediately. Unfortunately it did not work out. My unjustified reputation as a playboy would result in Henny's deportation. Henny had not been informed soon enough of my aunt's proposition and refused to marry me on the basis of my reputation. She wanted a man of her own, and not somebody who had a new girl almost every month.

I did not get a chance to explain to her that her view of me was totally wrong. Since it was harder now for the Germans to pick people off the street, a new system was used to get people to report for transportation of their own free will. Letters were mailed, and Henny was one of the first to report. She did not come back any more... And after all those years it still hurts to think I might have been able to save her if I had just talked to her.

In October 1942 the Jewish Council was ordered by the Germans to call all of the people who were unemployed to report for the 'Bosplan' – a work assignment program. Although it was prohibited to gather, lots of people were involved. One of them was my father. He was assigned to dig ditches in a project called the 'Amsterdam Forest' – a big park being developed at the edge of the city. Even though it was hard labor, my father seemed to enjoy it – at least he was safe from razias out there. But it was not long before everybody working on that site was sent to a camp named Westerbork. This was a 'distribution center' for German concentration camps.

It was strange to know your father was somewhere, but unable to come home. We were allowed to write and send packages and received letters in return. And when he wrote asking to help him to get out, because I was *sperred*, I took the bold step to go into the lion's den; the SS Headquarters. Here I pointed out that my father had been mistakenly taken to Westerbork and he had the right to be freed on my *sperr*. I did not realize that I went to their headquarters not wearing the Star of David; neither did they. I left with the promise that everything would be done to get my father released and they gave me the assurance that as long as the 'release investigation' was in progress, my father would be spared from transportation to Germany.

I went home to console my mother and took charge of family affairs for the time being. Here I was seventeen years old and at the head of the family. But it would only last a few months until it would be my turn to be picked up to spend the rest of the war in a variety of concentration camps. But before the time came, I would still go through some anxious moments.

One night, at about 8:30pm, our doorbell rang; it was not the way our family rang the bell. Either it was a stranger seeking protection from the Germans – a neighbor who defied the curfew and came via the fire-escape route to visit us, or the feared SS who came to get us. We became very tense and afraid. What to do? If it was the SS they would smash the door down anyhow. I went to open the door, and a man in civilian clothes asked me if there were any Jews living in our house. I calmly told him that he had picked the wrong address. Slowly, I closed the door and the man left. He turned out to be somebody from the German Security Police who worked in civilian clothes. We went to bed relieved, knowing we were safe for another day.

Another way we kept them from our doors was to obtain a sign from the Health Department stating our houses were unsafe because we were under quarantine. This scheme really scared the SS off for awhile. But it did not take them too long to ignore the signs and to find out they had been fooled. Another way to save ourselves from being sent to concentration camps was to be put in a hospital or a psychiatric institution.

An interesting fact; some people were released by bribing German authorities – which proves that even the 'Super Race' was corrupt. In fact some SS were corrupt enough to transport Jews to Switzerland in exchange for large amounts of money. My cousin was brought to Switzerland by the SS after paying $40,000.

In what is known today as the Czech Republic there was a special camp 'for the rich' by the name of TerezinStadt.

Inside TerezinStadt

Wealthy people who had been captured by the Germans would stay there with their entire family provided they paid a certain amount of money. They would be able to live in this so-called 'concentration camp' comfortably until the money ran out or until the war ended – which ever came first. And that is one of the reasons some families survived concentration camps. Even the head of the German SS, Mr. Aus der Fuenten had a couple Jewish chauffeurs working for him. Even though I do not think they got paid, they secured themselves a way from deportation.

In some instances, these people were able to get other individuals released in exchange for their services. So, instead of looking upon them as traitors, they were used to influence Aus der Fuenten to release people who were already captured.

Aus der Fuenten

In some cases, people were totally dependent on the SS' whims. And I am sure a lot of people paid for their good will only to find out, that release, was to be of a very short duration. Both chauffeurs survived the war along with their families and have lived with their misdeeds weighing on their conscience for the rest of their lives – hopefully they were long and difficult lives.

My Aunty Kitty who was only two years older than I, found a fellow by the name of Arie Cardozo and because he was a Portuguese Jew, my aunt was under the impression that he would be safe from deportation. My grandfather was given a weekend off from the asylum to attend his daughter's wedding. For safety reasons, the wedding was held at my grandparents' house. The whole family was there, and when we came in, we were lead past the most beautiful wedding cake I had ever seen. It was on display in the dining room. After everyone had a peek at the cake, the doors were closed and the celebration began. Everybody talked about the war and its predicted end.

Only my Uncle Michael was missing; he had been taken to Mauthausen with the first fifteen men that had been picked up.

Mauthausen Concentration Camp

Everyone avoided to mentioning him even though his wife and son were there. The bride and groom showed up a short while later. It was an impressive ceremony. My Aunt Kitty was dressed in a white lace wedding gown, and the groom in black. They looked like a happy couple to us. Then came the time to open the doors and bring out the wedding cake. The doors were opened, and there he was – my granddaddy, licking his fingers. How he did it, only Heaven knows. But there was nothing left of the wedding cake except the cardboard plate on which it had stood. This must have been my grandfather's biggest *holiday*. Nothing in his face showed that he was aware of what he had done. His holiday was very short though; the grand old man was returned to the asylum the next day only to die shortly afterwards without being aware of all the trouble facing his family. My Aunt's marriage only lasted one day. Arie was picked up the following day and sent to an 'extermination camp'. Kitty was left alone again with my grandmother. Even though they had a chance to go underground they decided against it and were picked up after a while to endure the same fate as all of the deported Jews.

People became accustomed to this way of life. Every day you lived in suspense – who would be the next one to be picked up? And yet every day that you were allowed to spend with your family was a precious one. To be picked up was like going into the unknown. If you only knew what your destiny held for you, it would have been easier to make a decision as to what to do next. Very often depression set in, and quite a few people committed suicide. But then, all that was needed was a bombardment by our allies to lift our spirits again. When we heard the bombers we knew somebody was flying for us – dishing out the kind of punishment we would have liked to impose on them ourselves but were unable to do so. And when they dropped bombs on our own country, they were bombs of hope for us. We even went outdoors during air raids to enjoy the sight and sound of 'freedom'. The most spectacular sight was when a German plane exploded on the ground – we greeted the event with loud cheers.

Once in a while you were reminded that underground resistance forces were at work as well – working for us. Signs such as a German soldier floating down our city canals, or a raid of the government offices showed that even though we were occupied we were not defeated. But always, there were reprisals; razias became part of our life. A knock at the door, usually after 8:00pm, meant that time had run out. You took your ready, packed suitcase and went along, hoping for the best – all of your belongings were left behind. If your friends and neighbors did not take off with your belongings, the Nazis did. Everywhere when people were taken away, the Nazis would send a moving van and ransack the house. This was called 'Palsen'; the name of the company who did the job. Everything acquired in this way was transported to Germany and distributed over there. When a moving van from Palsen arrived in front of a house, you could be sure that the family living in that home had fallen victim to the Nazi regime. It was a sad and frustrating time.

The Palsen truck took everything away...

CHAPTER IV

Camp life

The Costs of Survival

November 10th, 1942, 6:30am – the alarm clock wakes me up. Everything is quiet in the house; I hear my mother in the kitchen fixing breakfast. Slowly I get out of bed, careful not to wake my sister in the next room. The sun is shining, so I decide to walk to work; it is Friday, and a weekend lies ahead of us. At 7:30am I reach the place where I have to take the ferry for a ten-minute ride across the canal. Every day you see the same people going to work. Nothing shows this day to be different from any other day. At the plant the bell rings announcing the start of another workday. I start the conveyor. Only Kitty Green is missing, she is sick apparently. She is already being replaced by somebody else. Another girl is not present today – Martha Korthagen.

Martha had been picked up the previous night by the German Security Forces; accused of listening to the BBC radio program and had been held at the SS

Headquarters on Euterpestraat, for hours on end. We assumed that, under great pressure she had been forced to disclose the (non-existent) conspiracy at Hollandia; to accommodate the Germans and to try saving herself from deportation or worse. At 4:30pm the factory was surrounded by German Security Forces. If it weren't so tragic an event, it would have been comical the way they behaved; guns drawn and fighting helmet on their head, they came charging in and stopped the conveyor. No one moved; we were scared to death. Not a word was spoken until their commander came in – telling us not to worry! All they wanted was to arrest certain people who supposedly had distributed illegal literature. The ones not involved had nothing to worry about and would be released in a short while.

5:00pm – the end of another workday. The bell sounded telling us that we could go home. Today however, no one was allowed to leave.

At around 7:30pm, our names were called one by one and we were separated in two groups. The Jews were separated from the non-Jews; the Gentiles were allowed to go home. The officer in charge assured all of us left standing, that we would be released as soon as passes were issued so that we could go home safely after curfew. By now the tension was so palpable that you could have cut it with knife. Could we trust them? Maybe – they had respected our *sperr* for such a long time, and we, after all, were 'important' to them; we produced their uniforms.

It was getting dark; the curtains had to be drawn so that we would not be targeted during allied air raids. When I was ordered to do so, I decided to try my chances at freedom. I could escape through the backdoor (tucked away in a corner; out of sight) and make my way down the fire escape. Slowly I opened the door – all I had to do now was to run down the stairs and I would be homeward bound. I stepped outside into darkness only to find myself face to face with a German SS who threw me back inside. We were surrounded. No escape was possible.

The tension inside became unbearable. Some of the girls were sobbing uncontrollably and everyone was nervous to say the least.

At 8:00pm, we were led downstairs; at least we were moving – the long unnerving wait was over. Maybe we could get our passes and go home soon… But that wasn't to be. Our hopes were crushed when the front doors opened and we saw two big trucks backing up to the entrance. There was no doubt left in anyone's mind now – we were trapped. Within minutes we were shoved inside the trucks like herrings on a fishing trawler. I was one of the last ones to climb aboard, so I made sure I had a spot from where I could escape at the first opportunity. When we reached the ferry terminal, we were jolted backwards and forwards, so I tried another escape. I slipped from under the canvas cover, my feet touched the deck of the ferry – in a minute I would be able to disappear into the crowd. But…two hands grabbed my shoulders and pulled me back inside the truck. To resist would not have helped and again my efforts had been thwarted. We had reached the other side of the canal by now. Where were we going? What was our destination? We sped through town for about fifteen minutes while we were losing all sense of direction being driven like a bunch of cattle in the back of this truck. When we reached the SS Headquarters and finally stopped, we were herded inside where we were told that we were going to be sent to a clothing factory in Marienberg, Germany. We would stay together and work over there.

In the basement of the building we passed a window; I could barely see her but Martha was sitting beside a man who shook his head or nodded every time she pointed at each one of us. We were divided into two sections – a 'yes' and a 'no' section, depending on the man shaking or nodding his head. The 'yes' meant that the person had supposedly participated in 'the sabotage' and the 'no' meant the opposite. I was selected to the 'no' group. At the time however, we had no idea what it meant. Somehow everybody thought it would be better to be in the other group for no reason at all. We were questioned one by one about our knowledge of what went on at Kattenburg. After the questioning was over we were transported by the same trucks to the central railroad station.

When the truck stopped at the station's entrance, I took a peek through an opening in the canvas to discover one of grandfather's old banana trucks parked nearby; his former chauffeur was standing next to the truck. It was late at night – only a few people around. Maybe my old buddy would give me a helping hand in getting out of this predicament. I was sure he would not let me down. Slowly but decisively, I got down from the truck and walked to where the chauffeur was standing. He recognized me at once – but showed no surprise. I guess he refused to help me in order not to endanger his own life. He turned me down cold and without a word of explanation he walked me back to the army truck. He wished me good luck and disappeared out of sight.

Soon the trucks moved up the ramp onto the railroad station; they were posted close to the doors of the railroad cars and were ordered to get into them. The operation went smoothly; you could even hear sighs of relief coming from some of us. Somehow we knew that our next stop would be Westerbork, where I would be able to see my father; and we also knew our final destination... The train started rolling down the tracks on its way to Westerbork where we arrived at midnight. The train stopped inside the camp. The barbwire-gates closed behind us – we were fenced in now.

In need of a good night's sleep; we put out heads down wherever there was a place to lie down. And even though I was bone tired, I did not sleep a wink. However, the tension was gone; we did not have to worry about being picked up in a razia anymore.

Anxious to see my father, I roamed around checking out the facilities. Westerbork looked to me like a small city. People appeared at ease and not frightened. There was a post-office, theater, a mess-hall and even a food store where you could buy all kinds of stuff not available to us in the ghetto. The only drawback to all this shimmer was that you could not leave at will. The only ones working were the ones who kept the camp functioning. Everybody else spent their time waiting to be transported elsewhere. Our train was stationed outside the camp now lying in wait, like a monstrous beast, to take its prey to its lair. Yet I hadn't found my father – I didn't know how to go about it. But I guess people in the camp were just as anxious to find out who arrived 'by the last train'. And, it didn't take long for my father to find me. Boy was I glad to see him! He looked great. He worked as a cook in the kitchen, and it turned out he had been informed that he would go home soon because of my *sperr*. Nothing pleased me more than to hear the good news; I could take care of myself and with my father back home, he would be able to take care of the family. Since we hadn't had the opportunity to pack anything when we had been picked up at the factory, the first order of business was to get some clothes from home. A letter to my mother corrected this in a hurry. Of course she was overjoyed to hear that we were together and that we were okay. I spent three weeks at Westerbork, and although it was a 'concentration camp' it was a lot better than being chased through the city streets by the SS.

Westerbork distribution camp

During my time there, I saw very little of my father. He really worked hard all day long and he knew I was in good hands with the Piller Family, who adopted me as one of their own. Their daughter, Lenie, and I became very fond of each other and decided whatever happened, no one was going to separate us; we would survive the war together.

Every Tuesday and Friday a train-load went from Westerbork to Germany. Names were picked in advance. So, you always knew you were safe until the next transportation when your name wasn't on the list. On the night of November 28th, my name was posted together with all the other Kattenburg people. The previous day, the 'yes' people had been brought in to go with us the following day; they had been held in a prison in the city of Scheveningen under horrible conditions. They were cast as criminals because of their 'yes' status, which had been given to them at SS Headquarters in Amsterdam. The night before I was due to leave I went to see my father to discuss the situation with him. Whilst surveying the previous transport operations, I discovered that it wasn't very hard to escape. All you had to do was to walk off the railroad station platform into the forest, under the cover of darkness. My escape would most probably impair my father's release; therefore, we decided against my escaping at this point in time. Had I known what was in store for me during the following years, I would have neglected to discuss this matter with him. Now that I had decided to stick it out, I would have to try and make the best of it. I reported for transportation like a 'good boy' together with the rest of my friends. Lenie and I switched suitcases so we could stay together. I was of the opinion that, if I said we belonged together, they would keep us together. I did not know at that time that men and women were sent to different camps. The women were dispatched immediately to the gas chambers. The only women who survived were the ones the Germans used for fertility experimentations – to make them infertile.

It was a regular train...

It was a regular train, and everybody was able to get a seat. My father was waiting for me at the gate – to say 'goodbye'; the last one… I wanted to cry, I had to keep my composure to re-assure him that everything would be alright with me. I shot another glance out of the window; my father was still standing there watching the train. It was an eerie sight to seeing him, he looked lonely. There was still a chance that he could join me – if *they* were short one person on this load, they would add him to the count. They had to have the right amount of people when they left – orders were orders. Slowly, the train took off. I hoped to be seeing my father soon…

The mood among the passengers wasn't that bad, although everyone was quiet during the night and we all tried to get some sleep.

At sunrise the entire train came alive. We made breakfast with the food we had taken with us from Westerbork. Nobody wanted to talk about what lied ahead for us. It was a beautiful day. One of us started to sing old school songs and everyone joined in. Several times the train was side-tracked for hours. On the second day we passed a sign – it said "Minden". It meant that we had crossed the border and we were in Germany now. Suddenly our good mood dissipated. There was no more singing. As long as we were in Holland, we were in familiar surroundings; but now that we were in Germany, it seemed that we were not sure of our future anymore. We were heading towards the 'unknown'. Again the tension, among us, could be felt and cut through with a knife. Even the car-guards seemed more confident now. Once in a while when the old locomotive stopped to fill-up with water, and since that we were in Germany, we were allowed off the train to take a breather. But instead of feeling at ease, it was unnerving – we felt insecure and vulnerable.

Dead tired we arrived at Cosel. Three days and nights of traveling had broken our spirit; we had been led into Germany by cunning and with a lot of loving care so that nobody would try to escape! We had finally arrived – and we were too tired to ask questions. The place was lit by flood lights. Uniformed men were waiting outside on orders from their commander, Hauptfurher Lindner. They rushed the train, yelling out loud for us – men only, to get out of the train cars. I moved to leave the train but stopped for a moment and picked up Lenie's suitcase. I told the officer that I would not leave without Lenie. He grabbed my leg, pulling me off balance. I kicked him in the chest – which cost me dearly. A severe beating was the result of my impertinence. That was my first encounter with the German SS, a lot more of the same would follow.

We were told to sit cross-legged on the ground with our hands behind our head. The train then started rolling slowing down the tracks with the 'yes' people still on it – it was taking them to their final destination; the gas chambers of Auschwitz.

In Cosel we were loaded on trucks and moved to our first concentration camp – Akraw.

Things changed drastically now; we were scared to death. All we could do was to roll with the punches and try to adjust to the new conditions. You knew that from now on end you would have to follow the German's orders – yelled at you in German. A beating was yours if you dared telling the officers that you didn't understand the language. Therefore, the first order of business was to learn German; and quick!

From the outside, Akraw, looked like Westerbork; wired fences, watch towers manned by armed guards, flood lights all around to prevent any escape. Here we were to be prepared for our future life in hard-labor camps. But this was still an instruction camp and distribution center for other concentration camps. On little or no food we were greeted by prisoners who had been living in that camp for awhile and who warned us that all our valuables would be taken away from us. Even though we believed them, we were not about to hand our valuables to complete strangers without a fight. Some people hid their jewels inside their mouth and got away with it. As for the others, everything else of value was indeed confiscated. I had nothing to hide; all I had was a suitcase full of lady's clothing. When my suitcase was checked – it was given back to me; and I could see a strange look in the officer's eyes, 'What was I going to do with a case-full of lady's clothes?' So, for three days I was the 'camp jester' wearing women's frocks. But ultimately help came from my friends who were obviously aware of my somewhat embarrassing situation, and who gave me some of their clothes to wear. We kept our suitcases for about three days before they were taken away from us. We only held on to our forks and knives that we were given in Westerbork

Soon after our arrival at Akraw, I found a flourishing black-market operation which would trade goods with the outside world; our clothing could be exchanged for food… (But I did not get anything from Lenie's clothes, nor did I want to.)

We worked on the German Autobahn and our civilian supervisors would eagerly select our 'goods' at bargain prices. The way it worked is that when we worked with civilians; whatever we could steal we would sell for food – that business was called "boy steal, you pay;" (bouw stelle yopu)

Sometimes we worked on farms were we stole vegetables. My big prize was when I found tubes of toothpaste that were hidden in the camp which brought in a lot of food when I sold them to civilians.

One of our tasks was to fill dump cars with sand from a grove up on a hillside. The hard part was to push the cars up the hill to the place where we would fill them up. Loading sand was exhausting. But the most difficult and dangerous part of the job was to guide the cars downhill. They were mounted on railroad tracks. In order to slow the cars down, we would put a pole between the back and front wheels; and by applying pressure on the pole we would reduce its downhill speed considerably. On one particular day, when I stepped on the pole it cracked under my weight; I yelled to the people in front of the car to get out of the way, to jump aside – but they didn't hear me… We were gaining speed, faster and faster the car traveled down the rails, the end of the tracks was in sight – I couldn't think… My brain seemed to be empty. Panic didn't take hold however, for some reason I was calm, maybe I was numb – I don't know. Nearing the end of the rails at tremendous speed everyone on board jumped and rolled down the ditch ten feet below the car, which passed us on the way to its last stop and crashed at the end of the ramp. We escaped with only minor injuries.

Six weeks passed. We were ready for distribution now. Hanunschild, an officer who selected prisoners for distribution, was due to arrive in camp the next day. We called him 'The Slave-Driver' because he used to size up the prisoners and select them according to their strength. Weaklings were eliminated and immediately sent to extermination camps – on his sole order. Knowing the criteria leading to the selection, helped you in trying to make a good impression on him. I was selected to go to Spitzkowitz – but I didn't know it then.

This time we were transported in cattle wagons. When they closed the doors on us we felt trapped. We could only see the outside through some holes or cracks in the plank sidings of the cars. We stopped at Auschwitz – this was a place where no one wanted to go. From the car we could see the camp below the railroad tracks. If we were unloaded here the only way out would have been through the chimney smoke escaping from the gas chambers.

Why did we have to wait so long? Why did we stop here? These were thoughts that ran through everyone's mind. If this was it, there was no reason for us to wait… All of a sudden, the train started moving again – What now? Where were we headed? All we could do was to sit and wait for our fate – nothing would be worse than Auschwitz, was the consoling thought.

Soon we stopped at a sign which read Spitskowitz. It turned out to be a 'new camp' only half finished – no lights and *no water*. But, on the other hand it didn't look that bad – especially after seeing Auschwitz. It also felt comfortable not to see a gas chamber nearby; it was not equipped with one.

On the first night we were treated to sauerkraut with sausages. On the second night it was even better… What was this – a vacation resort? Even the guards were friendly old men; veterans of World War I. I found out later that this was an "SA camp". There were three kinds of concentration camps. The most common were the concentration camp controlled by the SS. The second kind was the SA camps – such as Spitzkowitz where we were now. The third kind was controlled by the army. How were they different? When you were under the SS you could count on daily mental as well as physical abuse. The SA camps were managed by veterans from the First World War and generally decent, the best was the army camps.

Further, I have to explain that none of the German officers were allowed to kill you, and they had to account for every one who was killed. The only way they could shoot you was when you tried to escape. Often they told you to run, and when you did, they killed you outright; they needed the prisoners because, all able German men were at the frontlines fighting. We were needed to carry out the chores…

Strangely enough we were not even fenced in. I guess we had made it! In such an environment, it would be easy to survive the war. Our hopes were smashed however only four days later – we were then moved to the worst camp anybody ever encountered – its name was 'Lazy'; a very deceptive name for a concentration camp. When I arrived, it contained *two thousand* prisoners – but in the span of three months only *seventeen* of us survived the ordeal!

On arrival we were counted and divided in groups of thirty men. Each group was assigned a barrack, and a commander was appointed to each barrack. He was called the Stube Alterste. He was in charge of the barracks' cleanliness. And even though he was also a prisoner, he had been chosen for his toughness and had the privilege of not working. He had his own room and was assigned a boy to take care of him and his room. Beating up people was his way of keeping his position and to stay alive.

Our Stube Alterste's name was William Sys. In civilian life he used to be a butcher. He tyrannized everybody under his command.

As in all camps, there was a pecking order – such as with animals everyone knew where they belonged. This was something I had not learned yet however. As a greenhorn, it was my opinion that we were all in this war together and that we should stick together to survive. So, when I was ordered to clean-up the spilled food (that had been spilled by someone else), I didn't object, but I intended to take my time doing it. When

I heard the order I was sitting on the top cot of a three-story bunk-bed.

Bunk-beds in camp barracks

Our Stube Alterste became impatient and quite upset when I refused to obey his order *at once*! He got so mad in fact; he had to show his authority – he rushed across the room, carrying a two-inch thick stick. It took me a split second to react – the moment the stick came down, I pointed my knife to meet the blow. He hit me with such force that when his hand struck the knife it caused him to lose his thumb! Blood was flowing everywhere – but I had no sympathy for him or any remorse. He was rushed to the hospital at once.

Deadly silence had filled the room now. What was going to happen next? It was not going to be possible to get away with this. It did not take very long for me to get the answer to my question. The door opened

and one of the prisoner yelled "Achtum!" – Two men
entered the room. One of them was the SS Camp
Commander. He asked for the one who injured the
Stube Alterste to step forward. There was a puddle
of blood at my feet; I couldn't deny my guilt... So I
stepped forward once again. The Commander looked
straight at me and asked how old I was. I figured it
would not hurt to lie a little; I told him I was sixteen
years old. His answer to that statement; was a verdict
of twenty-five strokes on my back and he pointed out
that I got off easy because of my age.

The first stroke felt like as if the stick was going
through me. The second stroke felt even worse. I bit
my lip not to scream. After the fifth stroke, I became
numb – I didn't feel the beating anymore. I passed out
and couldn't remember the rest of the punishment.

The next day was a very bad one. Yet again, my
fellow prisoners helped me through the day by hiding
me in a shack at our place of work.

Our job consisted in laying and replacing railroad
tracks and loading coal for transport to the front lines.
It was a very cold winter; most of the time it was
thirty below-zero. There was snow all around you –
everywhere you looked was ice, cold and snow. When
you picked up a track with your bare hands, it would
stick to your hand tearing the skin off. We worked in
such conditions for six days a week from 7:00am to
5:00pm with only a break for lunch which consisted of
a piece of bread and some ersatz coffee.

If you were lucky you were assigned to keep the fire going for the guards. And when you worked hard, there was always a chance you would draw a guard's attention on you and he would pull you off the job for a short break by the fire. At lunch we all crouched down around the fire to get a reprieve from feeling the frosty air lashing your skin. Frostbites were common occurrences, and we had to go through the excruciating pain of it almost daily – especially at night when your feet started to warm up. But we considered ourselves lucky enough – amputation from gangrene was another of the daily routines.

After work we were counted and marched back to the camp – most of us were heavier than what we were when we arrived in the morning. Pieces of coal were hidden in our clothes to supplement the small amount of coal allotted to us to keep our barracks warm. This was really a must if we wanted to stay alive. Without those few pieces of coal, we would freeze to death, literally, even in our barracks – and we no longer cared about the punishment if we were caught. During the night, we were assigned guard duty inside the barracks. Huddled close to the stove, two people sat on guard for an hour. I still can't understand why it was necessary to wake somebody every hour during the night to watch the stove glow. We never had a full night's sleep. Sometimes we were awoken in the middle of the night for a roll-call. We had to rush outside in the freezing cold, bare feet to be counted – just to disturb our sleep.

The camp was surrounded by high-voltage barb-wire fences – some prisoners desperate enough to commit suicide would throw themselves against the fences and ended it all. Yet, a few guys managed to escape by jumping into the wire and scaling it with great efforts. When someone succeeded and survived their escape, the rest of us were made responsible for letting them flee.

For hours we were put through strenuous exercises after a hard day's work. And if you were unable to continue, you were prodded by a guard to prove you wrong. Some died from sheer exhaustion or fright.

Death became a daily companion and affected you less and less. In the struggle for life, there was only one body that counted – yours. Of course you would always try to help your friends to survive and counted on them to do the same for you when the time came. There was no way you could survive by yourself. When somebody was so depressed that they discussed suicide, you tried to change their mind, but when the man was serious and determined to end his life, there was no way you could stop him from ending it.

This was the case with my Polish mate who confided to me that he was going to take his life at the first opportunity – when a train passed by. I did not take him seriously at first. But, sure enough, when the eleven o'clock train came round the corner and we all looked up to see if anybody would be so kind as to throw some food to us, my friend dashed forward. The train came to a screeching halt. But it was too late. His body cut in half, strangely twisted, yet alive, he uttered: "I told you so." A grin came over his face when he died – another victim of 'Lazy'.

One night three prisoners who had escaped three days earlier were caught. To scare us off, or deter us from doing the same thing, we were called to the prison's main square. Barrack by barrack, we were marched single file through a small alley to the flood-lit square. Three bodies were dangling from the trees – another victory for Nazi Germany.

Up to that point, we had been fortunate to be allowed to wear our own clothes. That soon changed. Every Stuby Arterste was ordered to appear with his people to receive the new blue and white striped prison uniform at the wash barrack. And to humiliate us even further our hair was cut one inch from our scalp with a band two inches wide shaven clean from the front to the back of our head. That would make us recognizable from a distance. We were now escape-proof.

One morning, from a pile of shoes we were allowed to select any pair we liked. Even though I am Dutch, I had never worn wooden shoes. But I knew they would protect me from cold and wetness, so I picked up the only pair from the heap – not knowing how they would save my life in the most unexpected way.

It had been a terrible night. Not only was it my night for guard duty, but after I had just fallen asleep, we were awoken for another roll-call. No wonder I was dead tired the next morning when I went to work. I was assigned to the railroad crew carrying railroad tracks. There were some skills involved in the process, which would prevent you from getting hurt. Each length of track was carried by four men – if you released the track at the same time there wouldn't be any problem.

Since I had a sleepless night, I wasn't paying attention, I wasn't alert and I did not hear the command to throw off the track. I held on and was thrown off my feet by the force of the sweeping track – I couldn't let go anymore. And as I fell, the track dropped on my feet smashing my wooden shoes. I didn't feel any pain; I was unharmed – God bless them.

An injury would have meant certain death – no mercy for a badly injured slave. Only when you had a fever, an exception was made, so that you could recover; you were allowed to do some light work inside the camp and return to your work after a few days. But there was always a risk involved in doing that – you may be discovered by the German Commander and transported to be exterminated; thus, very few people took advantage of it.

On that particular day however, a father and son were able to stay inside together and took the opportunity to search the camp. In the laundry room they found some nice shirts which they would swap outside the camp for food. Unfortunately they were caught stealing; their punishment was something I will never forget…

Each of them was given a stick and placed in the middle of the main square, surrounded by prisoners and guards. They were ordered to hit each other until one of them died. After hitting each other for about a half-hour, the father succumbed. The son survived the war and is still alive today.

To be put in such a position was a tragedy in itself. They had two choices. Either refuse and be killed by the SS or do as they were told and the survivor would live with the memory of killing the other for the rest of his life. I am glad I never had to make a decision like that, even though I know I would have chosen to die.

Events like that were just entertainments for the SS beasts. They would invent all kinds of torture to see how much one could endure.

One of those inventions was the 'cold shower'. That treatment was given to thousands of people who were either unable to do heavy duty work required of them, or to the ones who were near death due to exhaustion. The victims were led to the shower room, a fire hose attached to their chest with the full force of the ice cold water aimed at their heart. After fifteen or twenty minutes the heart would stop...

I was closely involved with this type of torture on one occasion when my willingness to help a friend would result in his death. It was a Sunday morning, the day of rest designated by our Creator. Even the Germans respected that day – except when a railroad car had to be unloaded. Then a company was formed to unload the car. That Sunday, a friend of mine was called for duty. He was so weaken that if he went to work he would not make it through the day, so I stepped forward to replace him when his name was called. It turned out to be a very unlucky day for him. Our group consisted of thirteen men. We had to shovel coal. Two men were assigned to a car. It made me the odd-man-out. Not knowing what went on in the other cars, I worked hard. When everyone was finished, I had only about one-third of the load left. The guard was so impressed with my work that he recommended for me to get extra food. Two others were also recommended. Back at camp we were called out of the line up to receive our reward. When my friend's name was called I did not dare to step forward because I was known to the Commander by name, so I pushed my friend forward. Everything would have been alright if the guard had not pulled him back and pushed me forward instead. I had to admit that I had taken my friend's place.

We were both led away to the shower room where he got the cold shower treatment administered by a little, fat criminal by the name Auerbach. And as for my punishment, I was put, with the corpse, in a cell for the rest of the night. This was too much for me, I cried all night. I had lost another friend – how many more would follow?

A while later, my job with the railroad came to an end. I was assigned to a brick layer as his assistant. My job was to hand him the needed bricks. Mr. Jonge was seventy years old and a civilian. He sympathized with my fate. Every morning he left me some breakfast. Too afraid to do it openly, he would hide it and would tell me where to get it. He never had a harsh word to say about anything. The poor man was told by his leader to hate Jews and he didn't know how to do that. He asked me what my occupation was and got very confused when I told him. He had been told that Jews were shrewd business men and bankers; it was hard for him to believe that I was only a hard working cloth-presser. And when he asked me to explain why Queen Wilhelmina felt Holland when the German invaded the country while King Albert of Belgium stayed behind;

I answered jokingly that our Queen was smarter and got to the plane on time! At hearing the answer, he got so mad that he said he would report me to the SS Commander. He was really old and confused... I told him that he was really a nice man; that he had children and grandchildren but that I was just a lonesome guy with nothing left in the world and bound to die anyhow. I added that when the Germans would kill me, I would be out of my misery and no one would shed a tear. "But what would happen to you? You might end up in the same place as I am now." My bluff worked, but would result in a completely different relationship between us.

Actually, an accident brought an end to our partnership. We were building a three-story factory designed for the production of army-tanks. He was standing on a scaffold next to the old factory and a tank below him was in the way. He explained to me how to start the tank and asked me to move it a bit. I revved up the motor and pulled some handles. The vehicle started zigzagging uncontrollably and suddenly it hit the scaffold. Slowly, I saw it collapsing – I was stunned and helpless. Mr. Jong came down with the scaffold hitting the pavement right in front of me. He groaned from the pain. I rushed to stop the tank and ran for help – I don't know how I did it, all I remember was seeing Mr. Jong on the ground lying at my feet. He was rushed to the hospital and I was told that he recovered from his injuries after a while.

Since I wasn't needed at the factory anymore, I was returned to the railroad crew. I knew the job, and even though it was hard, I could handle it without any problem. Until then I had managed to keep my strength, because I always supplemented my food supply by selling my weekly cigarette allowance. Some people died mainly because of their addiction – they preferred smoking to eating! They even traded their life-saving bread supply for tobacco. Nobody could talk them into quitting their habit.

Another way to get some extra food was a scheme which we called 'organizing it'. In our eyes 'organizing' to get food was different from 'stealing' it. Stealing was taking away from someone's daily ration. But if you could swipe his 'extras' or steal from the kitchen without being caught, that was called 'organizing' our supplements.

I also kept my spirits up by singing out loud. Sometimes this behavior attracted attention and a strange look in the eyes of my fellow prisoners. When you sang however, you had no time to think of your misery and you could even lift the morale of others around you.

Little things meant a lot – a piece of bread, a friendly smile, a good word at the right time gave you hope and courage to go on living. So, imagine what it would do to you when a guy appears like a 'white knight' and begins protecting you against your enemies. This fellow, this hero was Buby Rinner. Buby was Jewish, twenty-five years old and not impressed at all by Hitler's Regime. Before he came to camp we were terrorized by a Polish civilian by the name Gamzela. He could eat a Jew for breakfast and roam around the camp beating us for pleasure. Buby came to camp as a volunteer to be with his mother, who was one of the six women imprisoned at our camp. He had insisted to be taken in and his wish had been granted. He would become a very important man for most of us.

He looked vibrant and full of spirit. He was allowed to roam freely outside the camp from location to location, checking on the working conditions. One day when Gamzela was conducting himself like an animal again, hitting everybody in sight, Buby arrived in the nick of time. He looked Gamzela straight in the eyes and said; "You bastard, if I see you hit one of my people once more, I'll break every single bone in your body". The confrontation was witnessed by one of the guards who did not interfere and Gamzela backed off. He stood there totally humiliated in front of the people he despised so much...

I became Buby's buddy – he called me 'The Crazy Dutchman'. He introduced me to his mother, Mina Rinner, who adopted me as her second son. This marked the end of hard work for me – at least in this camp. I filled my day with cleaning rooms at the camp Commander's quarters and I was even permitted to skip roll-calls in the morning. I also got plenty of food supplements from the Commander for my services.

All of a sudden however, Buby disappeared – he went the same way he came. We were sad not to have him around, but he had done his job. Beatings at the job-site ceased and work seemed lighter somehow. But the one thing for which he couldn't do anything was the death count. Heavy work, weak bodies and little food took their toll. The death count took tremendous proportions. Our work projects seemed to come to an end – there were only seventeen of us left and there were no new arrivals. This spelled the end of 'Lazy'. The camp was closed and the detainees sent to another camp called Annenberg to be redistributed to other camps.

CHAPTER V
More Camps

A way of life

I was selected by 'Slave-Driver' Hanunschild to go to Ottmuth, which was known as a 'good camp'. A 'good camp' was a camp where you worked hard and did not get beaten to death. You only died of exhaustion or when you were mentally unable to cope with the situation anymore.

There were six girls living at the camp also. They were housed in separate quarters, and managed the kitchen. Without any sexual undertone, they would always select some guys as their favorites – they would take special care of the men they picked. I was selected as one of the lucky ones, and every night, after the kitchen was closed I would go back to get some leftovers. Often I would have enough to share with my fellow countrymen. Sharing food was the same as collecting IOU's for bad times to come. As fellows of the same country, you would band together helping each other to survive. At every opportunity we had 'pep sessions' where we talked mostly about the future – what we would do when we would return to our homeland. One of our favorite chats was to create imaginary dinners, with all the trimmings and our family sitting around the table. But we never mentioned a 'Liberation Date' – for us, 'Liberation' was always six months away.

Death meant only an extension of life – it was only one day ahead of us. Death had meaning only when someone, on whom you depended to survive, suddenly disappeared. Death had no degree, no ascension, no arrival, no suddenness – it was 'just not being there anymore'.

My job at Ottmuth was to split rocks with a sledge hammer. It was made easier when an old diamond-cutter showed me how to detect the grain of the rock. By hitting a stone dead-center, it would fall to pieces. So, my work became challenging and pleasurable. Not only that, but by hitting rocks and smashing them to smithereens I was able to release a lot of pent-up anger and frustration – often I took each stone as a German SS that I would blast under my hammer!

Next to ours was an adjoining camp occupied by Russian prisoners of war. We became aware that discrimination was running rampant among them also. They were divided into two sections; the White Russians and the Mongolian Russians. It became apparent that the Mongolians, even under prison conditions, were the White Russian slaves. They had to do the dirty work, like washing dishes and shining shoes.

We found a way to communicate with them using the few words we had learned – bread was 'kleba', cigarettes were 'papiroskas'. And little by little we were able to get some of their extra supply of food through the barb-wires.

A while into my stay at Ottmuth, I discovered that it was possible to be transported to a civilian hospital (or so I was told). Encouraged by the possibility of getting out, I went to see the camp doctor and explained that I had an ulcer. Faking the symptoms was made easy for me, since I had experienced the real thing before leaving Amsterdam. I was hoping that if I could go to a hospital for treatment, I could enlist the sympathy of the doctors or nurses and stretch my stay a while longer or perhaps even stay out of incarceration all together. I guess I didn't play my role well enough, because my plan did not work. The only good thing that resulted from this aborted attempt was to be fed bland, tasteless food and being put on easy work-duty.

For awhile, I worked at Otta, a shoe factory. Another assignment was to work with a gardener's assistant to help develop the city parks. That assignment was similar to the one I had with Mr. Jonge – working with a civilian boss again. Although a guard was sent to the site with me, I was often left alone. Strange looks followed me everywhere I went because of my striped uniform and my noticeably different haircut. But for me, it was an odd experience; to be able to walk down the streets, to take a peek at the inside of a house again and to see people sitting around the table having dinner, just as I was ready to go back to camp to eat a meager meal…I often wondered when it was going to be my turn again to live amongst a family.

Yes, all in all, Ottmuth was a 'good camp' – but nothing 'good' lasts for ever.

Ottmuth would be transformed into a women's camp. Forty men stayed behind to bring the camp into condition for the new 'tenants'. The rest of us was sent to Graditz where I encountered the worst sanitary conditions I had ever seen.

Water was available out of a well as was used for everything. The sleeping arrangements were so that you did not have your own bed assigned to you. The whole room was one 'three-layer-bed'. At night you needed to find a place where to put your head down to sleep. Blankets were non-existent and lice were plentiful. Washing up was done at a creek whenever you got a chance to get to it. And it was not uncommon to be called outside in the middle of the night for 'feet inspection'! For hours we stood at attention in the shivering cold just to have the guards check our feet – how ridiculous can one get when power inflates one's brain.

And for the first time in my life I was infested with lice – first ten's of them; then it was hundreds and pretty soon there were too many to count. I would kill as many as I could find, but they seemed to multiply faster than I could eradicate them. A lot of people got very depressed by this plague – for me, there were too many to fight, and apathy set in, they became 'docile' like a domestic pet and some even died…

This was as low as anyone could fall – to treat lice as pets! For this, the Germans despised us even more; yet somehow I enjoyed telling them that they were 'real German lice' – no imports, just true blue Furher's lice… when the guards were telling us 'to take care of our lice'! Actually they were scared to get close to us and become bug-ridden also. It got to the point when we were all loaded onto a truck and sent to a public bathhouse. Our clothes were taken away from us to be steam-cleaned. After a hot shower our uniforms (still damp) were returned to us – we felt as if we were re-born, all washed and dressed anew. And when it came time to return to Graditz – we didn't! To our surprise we were transported to another camp – Klattendorf. And surprises were not to cease on that day, upon arrival we were handed a whole (and I mean 'an entire') loaf of bread whilst being assigned to barracks as in the 'good old days'…

The work consisted of a variety of jobs: building a school for carpenters and brick-layers, railroad work, and the dismantling of shot-down airplanes to retrieve spare parts. I even managed to obtain to work as a nurse in the prison hospital. Part of my duty was to empty the cesspool into carts and push the carts over rough terrain to a place where we could dump the excrements. Since pushing a cart is much easier than pulling it, I chose to set myself behind the vehicle and push it. However, this wasn't the smartest idea I ever had because I was the first to get splashed with some of the contents of the cart while pushing it, over and through, the ruts in the road and coming back to camp smelling like a pig. But a bath and some clean clothes would soon fix that. To be inside was at least better than working outside the camp – I couldn't complain.

I was the only Dutchman in camp and not well-liked by the Polish prisoners. To them I was an 'outsider' – not Jewish enough because I didn't speak Yiddish (a tongue mainly derived from German mixed with something else…). It was a rather strange camp. The Polish prisoners were able to receive packages from home like we did in Westerbork. Besides which they received money and were able to buy their way out for the weekend to return on Monday!

There was an adjoining camp for women located next to ours. It was there that I met Lindner again; the Commander who had made the prisoners' selection in Cosel. He lived in the woman's camp in a villa with his family. Most of the time he was not in attendance so everything was peaceful and quiet. But when his return to camp was announced everything was cleaned, spic-and-span, on the double – just to please him.

On those occasions, when he came home, no one was allowed to stay inside the camp. So, I was put to work dismantling airplane parts under the supervision of a Czechoslovakian girl named Natatza. It was a delight to see all of those shot-down planes. I was even able to listen to the radio broadcasts and interpreted the news in my own way. Even though this was a nice job, and the living conditions were acceptable, when they asked for volunteers to be transported to another camp, I thought it was time for me to move on and reported for transport. I didn't want to stay too close to Lindner and I was anxious to see new faces – away from the Polish Jews.

The camp where I landed was named Gorlitz, after the adjoining city where most of the prisoners worked. From a distance you could smell the sauerkraut factories.

I was pleasantly surprised when I arrived at camp to see a lot of familiar faces. The Commander was a man by the name of Coeman – I had met him previously under favorable conditions. But the big surprise was still to come – reuniting with Ma and Buby Rinner. They picked me right out of the line-up and told me not to worry. It would be like old times. With them in charge, my protection was insured, and because Gorlitz was a hard-labor camp, I needed all the protection I could get.

The sanitary conditions were excellent. Never before were we treated to a hot shower and clean clothes once a week. Since I didn't want to stay inside the camp, I asked to be assigned outside duties. I was given a light job – transporting sand on a cart pulled by a horse. The loading and unloading was done by other prisoners. All I had to do was to drive the horse and cart through town. The horse was a gentle mare, and even though it was the first time for me to get close to a horse, it did not cause me any problem. The guard – always sitting beside me, was a veteran from World War I, and he didn't care about whatever I did, as long as I didn't try to escape. We would usually take a route that led us along a road lined with apple trees planted on the sidewalks.

On my first day out, some apples fell by accident in the back of the cart – I was allowed to keep them. So, the next day I got bold and hit some of the tree-branches with my whip and got more apples than the previous day. This was a good way to supplement my diet because fruit were non-existent in many camps. My friends at camp benefited from my good fortune as well – there was enough to go round. This assignment went on for awhile until a prisoner escaped while doing the same type of work. All things that are nice seemed never to last very long when you lived in a concentration camp.

The advantage in doing all these jobs was that I learned to do various things and became skilled in many trades. My next assignment consisted in roofing a factory with tar paper. My supervisor was an understanding man and not very hard on any of us. He, himself, had spent a year in jail as a political prisoner.

My companions and I had to cover six hundred square feet a day. At that rate, the job was not going to last very long. We stalled as much as we could, and even took time to sunbathe between roofs. But in a week the work was done, our sun-tanning holiday was over and it was back to ditch-digging again. It wasn't that bad however. Four feet deep was a safe depth in which you could hide and with all the dirt shoveling around you and a friendly warning from well-meaning guard in case of upcoming danger, you were 'on easy street'.

One day I had an opportunity to escape… Food deliveries were made to the camp on a regular basis. That morning, I noticed a car entering the gates bearing Belgian plates. Quickly, I made my way to the kitchen and managed to talk to the driver – he was Belgian and spoke Dutch. After a very short conversation he told me to hide inside the car and offered to take me out of 'Hell'. We drove for a half hour – I was out of 'Hell' but fear grabbed hold of my senses. I didn't know where we were or where we were going and I didn't know if I could trust the fellow. Suddenly I couldn't go on. I yelled at him to take me back. I was ready to beat him to a pulp if he hadn't turned the car around. He was furious and yet he got me back to camp – no harm done. If anyone would ask me today why I insisted to be returned to 'Hell', I would have to answer – "Fear of the unknown (again) made me do it". Besides which, dressed as I was, in striped uniform with that stupid haircut, I would have been picked up in no time and shot to death – or worse.

Swapping stories from home was one of our favorite pastimes. A young German soldier; one of the guards, often took part in our conversations. His name was Heinz; I could say that we considered him as a friend. But we would find out that we couldn't trust a guard – even a friendly one. On one occasion, we were talking casually and we teased him because he seemed to be in a bad mood. But we didn't notice that he was not only in a bad mood but that his all attitude had changed and that something was really wrong.

During the conversation my friend Metselaar showed me a picture of his wife and children – suddenly Heinz grabbed the picture and tore it to pieces. Flying in a rage and without thinking of the consequences, I called him a 'son-of-bitch'. His reaction was immediate; he lunged at me and struck me on the side of the neck with the butt of his rifle. I felt a shooting pain through my neck and my head – I couldn't speak anymore. What went wrong? It turned out that one of the civilian supervisors had reported Heinz to the Commander regarding his 'undesirable friendly attitude' towards the prisoners which resulted in Heinz being severely reprimanded. He was told to change his ways or else he would be sent to the Russian Front. Thereafter Heinz was re-assigned to another squad and we never saw him again.

My voice returned slowly – it took the whole of six weeks for me to be able to speak clearly again. This incident taught me a valuable lesson – even a friendly guard would become an enemy if his life depended on it.

I soon found another source of income. Whether it was accidental or not, one day we received hundreds of tubes of toothpaste among a shipment of supplies. This was extraordinary. We had never been supplied with toothpaste. So, it was decided to use them as bartering merchandise with the outside world. I got my share – forty tubes! That was a real treasure. Germans were ready to exchange almost anything for a tube of toothpaste – it had become so scarce. I asked Mrs. Rinner what she needed and put out the word.

Sure enough – in a couple days I found someone who was ready to make a deal. A price was set and the merchandise exchanged. Lucky for me, I was never caught, or I would not be able to relate this story today.

It is the end of 1943. Most people who are still alive now have gone through a couple of years of concentration camp and have adjusted to a life of confinement. As in an everyday society, the camp community comprised classes of people; the privileged people and the ordinary people. At the top of the heap were those selected by the Germans to manage the camp's daily business. This upper class had a good chance of surviving as long as their privileges were secured. Besides the camp commander and his cronies, the cook, the barracks commanders (Stube Alterstes) and capos (work commanders) had the best chance at survival. They were fed well and had little or no work to do. They selected the head of the laundry department and all of the 'inside people' needed to carry out the daily routine duties. But, the lives of 'inside people' depended largely on the upper class' willingness to keep them in that position.

To rule in the kitchen was an art in itself. As kitchen helper, you were told how to deal with the upper class. They did not have to wait in line to get their meals. They were served from different kettles than those reserved for the ordinary prisoners. We always had to make sure that, as kitchen aids, we didn't stir the content of the kettles too much, so that most of the meat would remain at the bottom of the pot. If we could keep it down we would be able to serve it to one of our friends when he came along to get his ration.

As for the 'capos'; they were picked by the Germans for their toughness towards their fellow prisoners, and because they were selected by the Germans, they felt so secure that many of them really took it out on the prisoners as if they were Nazis themselves. But when they were dropped because of an over-supply of capos, for example, most of the time they were unable to sustain themselves because they were ignored by the rest of us and were not used to hard-labor.

These were physically strong men, but their muscles could not help them when faced with mental abuse. Many people died from mental and emotional depression. Being constantly abased, degraded and mostly ignored, these people became withdrawn, hollow-eyed, and lost weight until you could count every bone in their body. Down to that level of depression, they could no longer walk and only shuffled their way slowly and painfully. We named them 'Muselmen'.

A Muselman was a person whose days were numbered. We became experts at predicting the day they would die. We would watch them closely so that we could snatch anything they own quickly the moment they passed away. Like vultures, we watched them, and in some instances they were undressed before their corpse was cold. Perhaps today, it seemed that we were ruthless, but a jacket or a pair of shoes for us meant a few more weeks of survival – and they didn't need these things where they were going.

The downfall of William Sys is a good example of how a prominent capo could go to pieces. As a capo he had terrorized many of his fellow prisoners for years. In Gorlitz he fell out of grace and was demoted to an ordinary worker because he had lost his thumb (thanks to me!) And since he had no experience in hard work, he was unable to keep up with the rest of us and got beaten every day by his former protectors; the Germans. To us, he was an outcast, and if we could avoid working with him we did so. In camp, he was ignored, neglected and he soon became a loner. After a few weeks of enduring the silent treatment, he succumbed. Nobody cared. He was the victim of his own behavior.

To describe the brutal punishment and tortures that our German tormentors invented and imposed upon us; would take an entire book. They were masters at cruelty which they used to entertain themselves – and us! On such occasions, all prisoners were called to attend the 'show'. You were not allowed to turn your head away from the scene of action. Disobedience would result in additional punishment being applied to the person involved. All you could do was to try and close your mind from what was happening in front of your eyes.

On a couple of instances I was unable to do so and vomited on the spot. One of these instances entailed a beheading. Imagine being lined up in front of a barrack facing a sort of hangar – the prisoner facing you, a chain thrown around his neck in a noose. The chain is attached to two huge doors. The Commander in charge of the execution yells out: "Achtum!" Everyone clacks their heels – that sounded like a gunshot. The doors then open slowly; you hear only a short gurgle, and the victim's head comes rolling at your feet. Deathly silence envelops the prisoners – I felt helpless… How could you digest such cruelty? Believe me it takes you days and nights to force it out of your mind.

On another occasion we were forced to watch three prisoners being run over by an army vehicle several times – back and forth. This kind of punishment was dished out directly by German SS. Besides those I mentioned and among many other cases, there were a lot of punishment ordered by the SS but which were carried out by others under their command. And for some it was another way to survive another day, not realizing their time to die would also come. And for all that, corruption ran rampant among the guards – when the needed a personal favor – such as getting a hair cut or their watch being repaired, they forgot you were a Jew.

Even though Germans were known for their organizational talents, they showed to be extremely inefficient in the management of concentration camps. The most efficient camps were run by SS, others were run by SA (security forces) – so, and in order to reassemble everyone under one more effective banner, the decision was made at the end of 1943, to put all prisoners under SS command. To us it made no difference, except that it meant we were to move again.

Kitlitzstreben; a beautiful name for a concentration camp which would become the graveyard for many people – a brand new camp located somewhere in the forest in Opper Silezië, was our next destination.

Three men dressed in immaculate horsemen's outfits were introduced to us as camp managers. They distinguished themselves from us inasmuch as they were non-Jews and they *definitely* dressed differently! They would run the camp – mafia style. The leader of the pack was Emil Supper, a maniac who had been sentenced to spend the rest of his life behind bars for killing his wife. In charge of the kitchen was Gustav Peterman; he had been found guilty of robbery… And Eugene, who became the administrator, had been sent to camp for embezzlement – the perfect crew to manage a concentration camp! The first order of business, soon after we arrived, was to take whatever we had left as personal belongings away from us – and of course, a roll-call was called to get acquainted with Emil and our new 'home'.

In his long-winded introductory speech, Emil pointed out that from now on were *all the same* – no more Jews, but *protective prisoners*. He demanded strict discipline and coherence. He was going, without any outside help, to make this camp the most beautiful place in the whole of Germany! In order to accomplish this, we would have to work on the 'beautification' of our camp after our return from our daily chores on the outside. Anything needed to do the job had to be *organized* from outside camp. Rewards (in the form of extra food and cigarettes) could be earned by the best organizers. But anyone caught stealing would be penalized mercilessly.

Instead of our names we were now given numbers – same as real prisoners. My number was *19251*. We had to announce ourselves using our number if we wanted to be 'heard' by our superiors. It sounded terrible *to be a number* instead of bearing a name. But the worst was still to come.

As bad luck would have it; Emil took possession of a front room in my barrack until the building of his villa was completed. Aside from Emil's nearby presence I had to worry about other things... Barrack no.8 was the self-proclaimed kingdom of a Frenchman who had been a notorious pimp in his previous life. He was able to impose his will and enforce his power on everyone around him – that with the willing assistance of his entourage of cronies. During my years of incarceration, I had learned to be very leery of these kinds of gangs. Having some mad SS at the command of the camp, and three gangsters managing it, and having a gang such as the French Pimp's nearby was all very worrisome to say the least. Actually, the gang could make it, of break it, for us.

Unfortunately for me, my bed was located on top of the Frenchman's bed. Every time I wanted to get to my bed, I had to ask for his permission to climb to it. When he denied me access to my cot, at first I took it in stride and waited patiently for his nod of approval...

One day, I ran out of patience – unfortunately for him, I lost my temper. I marched down the aisle and climbed into my bed not waiting for his permission – but trying not to disturb him; I didn't succeed... He grabbed me by the leg and pulled me down. Everyone's eyes were on me. I had no real hostility towards the man. But, either I responded to his assault now or accepted the abuse for the rest of my days in that barrack. So I pushed him forcefully towards the center of the room and told him to get away from me. He came running at me like a wild animal. He presented a wonderful target for me to hit. I struck him on the chin, and he wobbled. I had to finish the job or he would get help. Seething with rage, I lifted him and with a surge of adrenaline, fueling me with untold strength, I held him over the burning stove. If anyone had tried to interfere at that point, I would have dropped him – as sure as I am alive today. He begged me for mercy, which abated my anger somehow and, amid the silence that had fell upon the room, I put him down... From that day forward he behaved as the regular prisoner that he was, the same as the rest of us. And, lucky for all of us, Emil was not in his room when the incident took place; otherwise it would have meant trouble for both of us.

There were another five of my countrymen in camp, and even though we were not housed in the same barrack we formed our own gang – not to terrorize others, but to help each other through the days ahead. We stuck together, and because of the bond we felt between us, three of us survived the war. I am sure that without each other we would never have been able to withstand all of the troubles that were still to come.

With Emil on our side, so to speak, we would be able to get some favorable positions to help all of us. Emil had previously been in the merchant marines and had had some good experiences during his stop-over in Holland. Jokingly he called us the 'Chocolate Munchers'.

He put me in charge of the potato-peelers; we were to make sure to have enough potatoes ready by cooking time. There was no pressure and plenty of food. Even though Gustav was in charge of the kitchen, Emil's presence was felt everywhere. When he found something not to his liking he would go berserk. On such a day, he could make it very hard on each and every one of us.

He showed no mercy towards anyone – not even towards the muselmen in camp. Although he was not allowed to kill anyone directly, many prisoners became victims of his rigorous exercises when he was in a bad mood.

We did everything not to wake him when he was asleep in the adjoining barrack. But once in a while we did not succeed, and then all hell would break loose. He even went as far as throwing an ax across the room – hitting our Stube Alterste. The man collapsed unconscious – this incident brought Emil to his senses instantly. If the guy was to die, he would have to explain the cause of death and would therefore be in real trouble. The camp doctor was called in immediately and the patient transferred to the hospital barrack. Emil went to see him almost every hour on the hour. After a few hours everything seemed to take a turn for the better – and Emil returned to being his old miserable self again.

It seemed strange that a life had so much value at one time, while at other times it had no value at all. The reason for this was perhaps because one had to make a distinction between able bodied men and those people who had become zombies because of the war. Most of the German able bodied men were in one of the services – the rest of us were badly needed to keep the German economy going. In fact, it all came down to one thing – if an able-bodied man was killed, it was strictly for punishment.

One morning Emil must have gotten up on the wrong side of the bed. He came charging in for a barrack inspection and found everything meeting his glare to be wrong. We were all lined up in front of our beds; you could see anger flaring in his eyes. He was in a bad mood – for a change! He looked at our beds and found they were not made up to his liking – blankets were not tight enough. Then he proceeded to topple all the beds over, ripping the mattresses open and spreading the straw over the floor. When he was done with his little temper-tantrum – he marched out; but not before telling us to have our room in ship-shape within ten minutes and ready for another inspection. We worked like hell to avoid his punishment – which we knew could be severe. We were very tense and awaited his return completely terrorized – but he never came back that day to inspect the room.

Roll-calls were something a concentration camp could not do without. Twice a day the SS Commander would come around to check on his flock. Our clothes and faces had to be clean and our hands came under close scrutiny – both sides. Such a roll-call could take up to two hours. All that time we had to stand at attention and looking straight ahead. The Commander would peer into your eyes, and if he saw something he didn't like, he would kick you in the shins with his boot. In case you felt the urge to change your facial expression because of the pain, all hell would break loose – again. Emil, who was usually standing beside the Commander, would order you to get down on all fours and start doing pushups until he would tell you to stop. Whenever you dared stopping of your own accord, he would lift you up and roll you over in the snow (or in a mud puddle; depending on the season) and jump up and down on you until you were soaking wet. When he was finished with you, you could return to the line-up and stand there at attention, for the duration – in the freezing cold.

The Commander was such a beast that his behavior drew the attention of the civilian supervisors. We often returned to work on Monday mornings bruised and crippled – sometimes hardly able to do our work. Since the SS Commander was paid by the civilian supervisors for getting able-bodied men to work in their enterprises, they sent a complaint to the Camp Commander at Gross Rosen – who was his superior officer, and asked that he would be replaced. As a result our Commander was fired and replaced by a young bachelor who turned out to be even worse!

All this new comer could think of – was to avenge his predecessor. So, the injuries continued to be inflicted. Our camp doctors, who were prisoners also, and MD's in civilian life literally performed miracles. They worked under the most difficult conditions with hardly any medicine available to them. Personally, I have seen and helped them when they amputated legs and arms which were gangrene infested or frostbitten. Most operations were conducted with a regular saw and by candlelight. Bandages were not available, so toilet paper was used to stop the bleeding. It was amazing that people would survive such operations with no anesthetics... They used alcohol to inebriate the patients and to some extent, ease their agonizing pain – but all that amounted to naught. Who ever survived such an amputation was doomed to die anyway; he became worthless to the working process. You have to ask yourself if it wouldn't have been better to let them die on the operating table...

Emil's wish to finish the camp's 'beautification', in six weeks, proved to be a pipe-dream. He soon realized that *his* goal would be difficult to reach and would be a 'perpetual job' for him. All material needed had to be 'organized'. Very often he would order to have a room painted in a particular color, but even before it was done, he would change his mind and another color would have to be applied over the first coat. This occurred primarily when it came to paint his house. It was going to be his private palace – but he would have to share it with Gustav, Eugene and his staff, including his friend and companion; Joseph.

Emil, who was, besides everything else, a homosexual, had picked Joseph as his mate. Joseph was a real nice boy about nineteen years of age and not a homosexual until Emil got his hands on him. I think he gave in to Emil's advances in order to survive... how wrong he was...

I was added to the outside work-crew, because of the shortage of able-bodied men. Thus, I was taken off the potato-squad and sent to Muna, a factory producing bombs. We were given the job to load the bombs on trucks. Four men had to load five-hundred pounds bombs by hand. One of the boys bragged that he would be able to carry one bomb all by himself if we would just put it on his shoulders. We lifted the bomb and sure enough he took a few steps on his own… But we quickly relieved him of his dangerous load and complimented him on his feat. He really did it! Well, if he could it – so could I! I gave it a try. The bomb was lifted on my back but when my companions let go of the load, I fell – there was no way I could do it too… Luckily there had not been any fuse in the bomb, and we had not thought of the danger beforehand. How stupid could one get? Or was it that we really didn't care anymore?

When more people were available again, I was taken off the outside work-crew and Emil promoted me to manage the laundry room. In that position it was very easy to earn extra food – I just had to take care of the VIP's laundry and delivering it to them personally. Besides which, I helped Joseph – Emil's factotum, as much as I could with jobs he didn't care to do. I had the added advantage of not being involved with Emil's punitive exercises when he was in a bad mood – he would announce in advance what he planned to do to us and I stayed out of his way. And I was able to inform my friends of the upcoming 'events' and they were able to dodge him as well. When roll-call was called we would avoid Emil by looking busy – we would run up and down, carrying tools and making sure he noticed us doing it. Actually we were not working, hardly at all. But you were never totally protected. When you fell into disgrace – for one reason or another, the penalty was severe.

A good example of this was Eugene' story (our administrator); he had been sentenced to hard labor and had already served eleven years. So when he was called to Gross Rosen (which was the headquarters for all four (or five) surrounding camps), we thought the lucky son of a bitch was finally going to get his release. Two days later two other prisoners, who had been selected by Emil, were also ordered to go to Gross Rosen.

Gross Rosen entrance block

They returned the same day. They had been called to witness Eugene's hanging and report this event to the rest of us. We didn't know what Eugene's crime had been but we assumed that he had fallen back into his old habit of fiddling the books and was caught doing it. Nobody cared – we wished those three gangsters the worst of luck.

These three would tyrannize us mercilessly at will and we were powerless to respond. Now there was one less to worry about. This incident must have had an effect on Emil as well; he must have realized how vulnerable he really was. And for awhile he acted more reasonably (for him), but we knew it could not last.

Finally Emil's house was finished – that was a relief in itself! It really was a small palace after all – it had all of the comforts, plus, what most houses didn't have.

Being working in the laundry room, you were known of all the VIP's because of all the special favors you would do for them. Their clothes were kept apart from others and pressed.   Besides receiving extra food, you also collected IOU's. The regular prisoners' clothes were cooked in big kettles to exterminate lice – and believe me I cooked a hell of a lot of lice to death...

Before being posted to the laundry room, I would try to kill as many lice as possible between my fingernails before I went to sleep at night – this was a necessary chore if I wanted to have a good night's sleep. But you were never able to kill all of them – so you had to content yourself with their presence and take the attitude they were not important. To some extent being covered with lice day in and day out was more humiliating than getting scolded or beaten.

My friend Hans was one of these people who suffered terribly from being infested with these dirty little tics... Coming out of a middle class, conservative family, he felt so humiliated that he almost went crazy.

So, when he gave up on killing lice and with it gave up on life we took turns helping him as much as possible. And, I am sure he wouldn't have been able to survive that ordeal without our help. He would have died mentally. But as soon as I was able to clean his clothes and change them on a regular basis you could see him coming back to life.

Nevertheless lice were here to stay, until the end of the war. You had to learn to live with them.

We, Dutchmen were lucky to have plenty of food because of the positions we occupied on the inside. Not so lucky were the guys working on the autobahn project. The only way for them to get some extra food was to beg or steal valuable articles and sell them for food. When caught, such a prisoner would be handed over to Emil, who would enjoy the punishment he inflicted, immensely. As I mentioned previously, it was not for stealing that you were punished, but for being caught doing so.

Matcek, a Polish prisoner, was caught stealing a German officer' shirt and handed over to Emil. The sentence was hanging. A scaffold was built, and the show was on. It was not an ordinary hanging, but a particularly Machiavellian one – devised by Emil himself. A rope was put around Matcek's waste and he was lifted to a foot above the ground. Nobody knew how long he was supposed to hang in this position, except Emil. He was exposed to the elements, and in order to slow the process, he was allowed to rest for short periods of time. No guards were assigned to him – escape would be impossible anyway. For me, it was the perfect opportunity to obstruct Emil's demonic design. I knew that if I were caught, my life would be over. But, it was worth the try. The first night, I checked the surrounding for danger signs. And when I judged the place to be relatively free of curious onlookers, I approached Matcek. At night he was allowed to sit or even lie down for a while – although his arms and legs were still bound. I told him of my plan and asked him how we could help him. He told me that even though the hanging was very hard, he felt he could beat the sentence, if we were to give him some food because he was only given one meager ration per day. I promised him our support and hoped he would not betray us under duress when questioned by Emil. I got together with our clan and told them of my plans; all I wanted from them was some extra food. For the rest, I did not want them to know what I was doing, so they could not break under the pressure of questioning.

In the middle of the night I went to see Matcek and was able to feed him an extra ration. That show of compassion on our part lifted his spirits a little – he appreciated the fact that he was no longer alone. The chance of being caught was very slim because our lavatories were located near the center of the camp and close to the scaffold where traffic was quite heavy during the night.

Emil must have felt that something was afoot because Matcek was still alive and actually was enduring the torture quite well. One night I almost ran into him, but for all of his searching and questioning I wasn't caught. Matcek did not talk – even after being repeatedly beaten severely. So when the excitement subsided and Emil was at the end of his teeter – and since he couldn't kill him outright, he had to release the prisoner. I felt a tremendous sense of satisfaction and relief; we had been able to save a life at a time when life was worth less than the dirt under the sole of your shoes. But I was to regret my good deed at a later stage of the game. As far as I was concerned, it wasn't me who saved Matcek – it was an act of God.

For some of us God played a role we had a hard time understanding. He, God being present or absent, or existing or not were daily topics of discussion – particularly during religious holidays. We had a Rabbi and a Catholic priest in camp. The priest was a Jew converted to Catholicism – yet he was considered as a full-blooded Jew by the Germans. Those discussions were heated ones to say the least. If God existed, how could He allow a thing such as this war to be cast upon us? And believe me this question was never answered to our satisfaction. Another question was whether or not we should observe Lent during our religious holidays in view of the conditions in which we lived. Observing Lent for us would mean death, and since our Jewish beliefs tell us that life is primordial, we were released from observing this fasting holiday. As for the question as to why we had to suffer so much it has never been explained to my satisfaction by any religious leader to date.

Camp life is a day to day proposition which changes without notice. One day Joseph came to me and asked if I would take care of Emil for a couple days while he went to hospital for treatment of some kind of infection.

I accepted, of course, and I found myself being closer to the 'top' than ever before. Cleaning Emil's room was not very difficult. It took a couple of hours, and the rest of the day I would spend it reading. Meanwhile I had the opportunity to find out what kind of person Emil really was – indeed, who was he? He was vain and self-assured – proud to talk about himself at length. While talking about his accomplishments, he showed me some sort of a safe which he had placed in the attic of the house where he kept the gold and jewelry he had confiscated from new, incoming prisoners. He called it his 'retirement security' for after the war. He had no misgivings about his future life – he was actually thinking the prisoners would leave him be after this was all over! And, when Joseph returned three days later and I was sent back to the laundry room, I knew more about Emil that was good for him. The information I had gathered would allow me tremendous protection in a confrontation I had with him later on.

Our daily routine had resumed upon my return to the laundry room. As Dutchmen we were able to delegate the dirty work to other inmates. We hired them to make our beds, to be on guard duty, and to perform all sorts of jobs which we didn't care doing. We could afford doing this because of our positions and the over-abundance of food we enjoyed.

However, there were things you had to do yourself whether you liked it or not – such as going to the lavatory. This presented no problem during the day since everyone was at work – but during the night it was another matter all together. We could not help going to the 'john' at night because of the watery food we ingested every day. It was a communal lavatory. There were two big beams stretched across the room on either side of the central cesspool. The gap between the beams was minimal – you did whatever you had to do sitting cheek-to-cheek and back-to-back. Sometimes a prisoner would doze off and fall backwards into the cesspool. And sometimes, after trying to rescue the guy from a suffocating death and after exhausting efforts to pull him out of the stench, you would discover that he was dead already… And even when everything went as planned and you had done what you had come to do; you still had to run back to your barrack in the freezing cold in your birthday suit, a blanket wrapped around you. Not a pleasant experience for anyone, especially when you had to go through it night after night.

A very important twist of fate would change my relationship with Emil. I was called back into service as Emil's factotum. Joseph had to go back to the hospital again; it was obvious just by looking at him that he was not going to make it… He died a few days later fallen victim of an infectious disease. A permanent replacement was needed, but I did not think I would be the one to extent my services beyond the call of duty. Emil however, had very different ideas on the subject.

I started my routine at Emil's house as on previous occasions – I cleaned his room and when that was done, I would set myself on an 'easy-chair' and would read one of Emil's books for the rest of the day. At about 5:00pm on that particular evening, Emil invited me to have dinner with him so that he would not be 'lonesome' – he said. To have dinner in pleasant surrounding was a treat I wouldn't pass up – so I accepted the offer. I ate the best meal I had had in years; at the end of which I felt replete (I had forgotten how it felt to eat to my satisfaction). As far as I was concerned this way of life could last for ever. After dinner Emil finally broke the silence and said: "Well, Lou, what are you going to do tonight?"

"Well," I replied, "I am going back to the boys in the barracks and I'll see you back here in the morning."

His next question really took me aback – I was shaken. "Why don't you stay over and sleep with me?" He asked a devilish smile coming across his face.

It was decision time for me. Without thinking, I said: "Emil, you're a nice guy, but your proposal is out of the question."

He looked at me calmly and said: "You understand what this means don't you? From now on somebody else will have to take your place – you will not be needed anymore".

And without further ado, the next day my job at Emil's was assigned to Andries – another Dutch fellow. Although there is no way for any of us to prove that he gave in to Emil's demands, he stayed on the job until we left Kitlitzstreben. He fast became a rosy-cheeked, chubby, roly-poly boy. He was very good to all of us Dutchmen and did us many favors. He survived the war apparently without doing any harm to himself or to others.

But this incident had further repercussions on me and my work. It resulted in my losing my job in the laundry room. A couple days after leaving Emil's place I was told to report the next day for duty at Lystikof, a road building company. This kind of revenge from Emil; I didn't quite expect. And I couldn't very well let him run my destiny like he did that of many others on numerous occasions – I decided that I would blackmail him instead!

"Emil," I said, "if this is your revenge, I advise you to stop right here and now. The next move you make against me, I'll take a particular pleasure in reporting your hidden treasure to the Commander. And, don't forget what happened to your friend, Eugene…"

However, he didn't give me the benefit of an answer – he turned on his heels and left. I guess he was satisfied with what he had accomplished – frustrating me.

So, it was back to outside commands again. Our supervisor, a man named Patcek, was another one of these people who enjoys his job while beating people for a hobby. An enemy like him was all that was needed to make life even more miserable than it already was. He was a first class slave-driver. If you dared to stop only to take a breather, you would regret it for the rest of the day. This situation didn't trouble me too much however. I was still able to work hard; and when you worked hard you would forget your sorrows for a while. It wouldn't be long before I was picked up by a surveyor to help him in his work.

Even though I was not part of the inner circle anymore, I had collected enough IOU's and sympathy from others that my food supply was secured for a long time to come. Work is something I have always enjoyed, but forced labor after a hard day's work was something I tried to avoid. At five o'clock we would march back to camp, collect our food ration and wash ourselves to look half-decent for the roll-call at six o'clock; which was usually conducted by Emil.

Tonight however, he was accompanied by the SS Commander. The purpose of this unexpected visit was to tell us that he needed volunteers to undertake the building of the camp expansion. The job would have to be done after work – of course, and an extra hour wouldn't hurt us any! Nobody showed any interest in the plan and didn't step forward. So, Emil had to pick the crew. I was the first man he picked – again I didn't expect his reaction. I don't know if he realized what I could have done to him – I just don't know what went through his mind, or was it that vanity made him forget how vulnerable he was? There was no way for me to refuse the call in front of the Commander. But I figured that if I went tonight, it wouldn't be my turn for a while to come. They only needed ten men. But lo and behold, the next night I was picked again. It was obvious that Emil was after me since every other man was different from the previous night. And when on the following night, the Commander asked for volunteers, I stepped forward! After volunteering three nights in a row, the Commander himself refused my assistance and sent me back to the line-up. He told me that I had done my share, and, Emil was defeated in his purpose. There was nothing he could do against the Commander's orders. Emil struck out. Not only was I noticed by the Commander, but now I would be recognized as a hard worker. I could not be punished for laziness any more – and that for as long as we had the same Commander at the head of our camp. The other benefit, which was not negligible, was the fact that I could approach the man to talk to him if I wished to do so.

I considered that I had shown enough patience thus far and that the next time Emil would try to put one on me, I would spill the beans and bring troubles to bear down on him. I was sure that, for a crime like the one, he had committed, of misappropriation, his head was already on the chopping block.

All the indications showed that there was a new transport due in pretty soon. Everything was prepared to receive the new comers. This meant that Emil's empire would expand and by the same token his wealth would increase as well. The new comers turned out to be Hungarian Jews, fresh from home – a gold mine for Emil. Their luggage was left at the camp main square, while they were guided to the bathhouse where they showered and were given their prison uniforms. When they returned to pick up their suitcase, they found that they had been thoroughly ransacked by Emil and his crew.

Among the new prisoners there was a little guy who started asking around if there were any Dutchmen among us. His name was Johnny Bussnach, or fondly called 'Pipo-the-Clown'. When we showed our colors, he assured us that we had no longer anything to worry about (!) since *he* had arrived at our camp. He said that he used to be a clown with Circus Bever in his 'previous' life and that he had performed successfully at every camp where he had been transported.

Performing for prisoners as well as for the Germans, this little guy sparked excitement and hope in all of us. And his good humor rubbed off on everyone who associated with him. He soon suggested forming an entertainment group to give Sunday performances.

Normally Sunday's were spent resting and talking about the future. Food sessions were often prominent in our conversations. We imagined being served the most delicious meals. But strangely enough we never mentioned our families. Maybe we were afraid to recall-to-mind, unwanted emotions. I, for one, was confident I would eat more chocolate bars when I returned home. Why? I don't know. Maybe it was because chocolate had not been available for years and I craved it. So, and until Johnny's arrival every Sunday was the same as the next.

But now we were going to be involved in Johnny's act. That meant we would be busy all of the time. We began with one act sketches. A room in Emil's quarters was given to us for rehearsal – next to his bathroom where we were able to take a hot shower after rehearsal. In one's of Johnny's acts, he pretended that he hypnotized me; he would order me to dip my finger in black shoe-polish and smear it on my face. At rehearsal everything went off smoothly and I was able to remove the shoe-polish without difficulty in a hot shower. On Sunday it was our 'Premiere'. It was a fantastic success. Lou Emmerik sang and tap danced. And our act received tremendous ovation – there was laughter all around. But now it was time to wash up and get our extra rations; to our surprise there was no hot water in the showers. It would be impossible to remove the shoe-polish with cold water, no way of getting my face cleaned before roll-call and no way Emil would let us use his shower. He had hoped that I would be punished for not having my face cleaned at roll-call. But, when the officer looked at me, I saw a big grin coming across his face… He moved on and didn't say a word. After roll-call, we warmed some water on the stove and took care of the problem quickly.

Since we were located somewhere in the middle of nowhere, the German's only form of entertainment was what we could offer them. Pipo's imagination was put to the test; he thought of every sort of distractions, one of them being a soccer game, detainees against Germans.

Where could we get another chance like that? We could play them hard but fair and dole out some punishing blows without fear of being punished. Winning the game was not that important to us, but if we were to beat them, it would be an added pleasure. When the day of the game arrived, we played hard – believe me. In the end we went back to our barracks quite satisfied with our performance.

We were the hero's of Kitlitzstreben – ready for the anticipated revenge, which however, never materialized. Some of our German opponents had not been able to report for work for a couple days after the game because of the bruises they had sustained in the middle of the action. The only regrettable result out of this was the next game being cancelled by the SS Commander.

The new Hungarian prisoners were no asset to our community. We were old timers, hardened through the years of hard work. We had adapted to the rigorous way of life. As new comers, they, on the other hand, had no time to adapt; they were put in a position where they had to do hard labor right from day one. And, of course, Emil didn't miss the chance to make 'model prisoners' out of them. They were treated to extra disciplinary exercises at every turn – many of them died of exhaustion, or Patcek would take care of beating them to death at work. No Buby Rinner here to help them. Their corpses were left piled up outside a barrack until there were enough of them to warrant a transport to Gross Rosen for cremation. Normally it would only take a couple of days to fill a quota. We, prisoners, were the ones to pile them on the trucks. Even though we did not like that sort of work, we felt nothing towards these dead men – as long as they were no friends involved, it did not affect us in the least anymore.

One good thing came with the arrival of the Hungarians; they had given us some relatively fresh information about the war and we learned that things were not going well for the Germans. That news alone was all we needed to hold on a while longer.

Autumn had arrived, and with it another cold winter was due. But in a way, and funny enough, as Jewish prisoners we really looked forward to Christmas. To us Christmas meant two days off and some really decent food. But this time Christmas would even be merrier.

Johnny was called in and ordered to organize a big variety show. We were told that everything would be supplied – costumes, stages, the works. The performance was to be conducted by the Dutchmen, and accompanied by some other prisoners who could play musical instruments. These guys formed a real band, they sounded very good. Also included in the show was Erwin Backen Roth – to play the part of 'Lily Marlene'. He was kind of girlish and perfectly suited for the part. All of us were given time off for rehearsal when needed. As a result, we were on 'easy street' again at least until Christmas.

The performance turned into a smashing success. After which we were complimented by the Commander and asked to come up with a similar show for the New Year's Eve Party. We were ever so glad for the assignment. However, we didn't know that the Commander had not informed Emil of his plan. And so, when we began our rehearsal the next day, Emil stormed in and destroyed all props and cancelled the show! How he explained *his* cancellation of the show to the Commander, I don't know – but the show was off.

Two kinds of diseases took a heavy toll on the prison population. Diarrhea was one of them and our lavatory being so far out of reach; it was a particular problem for the prisoners suffering from this affliction. In their weaken condition, some inmates were unable to leave their beds… The awful result being of course, that we had to sleep in a barrack that reeked like a cesspool. The worst part of this, for us, was that we had to make sure Emil or the Commander would not get a whiff of the stench, which permeated the barracks, during their morning rounds. So, in the middle of the night we helped the poor fellow as much as we could. We would clean and refresh his bed, put some new straw in the mattress and washed and dried his clothes overnight. To try curing this affliction we used to cook potatoes until they were burned to a crisp and fed them to the patient. This usually resulted in his recovery in a couple of days.

Dropsy was a disease that took its tool in every part of the prison community. Even privilege men with access to good food (by prison standard) succumbed to the disease. Every night when you went to bed, you wouldn't feel your legs for water. A sure sign that you were in trouble, was to press a finger on your leg and if the flesh didn't pop back instantly you could safely conclude that you had Dropsy. Hans was one of us who was afflicted and diagnosed with the disease. His legs were about twice the normal size; he could hardly walk but his mind remained as sharp as ever. His condition would actually save his life later on.

It was January now. We did not work outside anymore because of the onrush of Russian forces apparently surrounding the camp. Rumors had it that our camp was encircled with bombs ready to explode the moment the guards were ready to flee. A blueprint of the bombs fuse connections was supposed to be kept in the camp Commander's office. If we were able to get at it, Hans, who was an electrical engineer, would be able to cut the circuits before they did any damage. And this was when, for the first time, Emil gave us a helping hand. He was the only one who had access to the Commander's office. First we organized watch crews round the clock to alert us when the guards at the Commander's quarters would go for a break. Once inside his office we would have to find out if the plans really existed and take them. Once we knew the coast was clear, Emil called the Commander to a meeting to check on the connections between the camp and his office, and while the Commander was away we indeed found a blueprint, took it and brought it to Hans. I am sure Emil helped us to save his own skin – besides, if the disappearance of the blueprint was discovered it would have come down to me, and no one would have dared pointing the finger at him.

January 24th, on my birthday, a roll-call was called at 11:00pm. I was sure this was not done to celebrate my birthday, but there was no mistake about it – this was not a normal roll-call. The camp Commander was there and told us we were going to leave the camp on foot to travel to our new camp. The sick and dying would be left behind; now we were sure the sick would be destroyed. And Hans was one of them. Whatever it would take we would not leave him to his fate in that hell-hole. We even carried him to the camp square and held him standing at roll-call. He fainted and collapsed at our feet – we had to accept the fact that he couldn't travel with us... After being lined up for a couple of hours the trip was suddenly called off – suspended for the time being.

Three weeks went by. Our days were filled with playing cards. Unsure about what would happen next we knew the end was in sight. But how would it end? We hoped to be liberated by the Allied Forces, and, if possible not by the Russians. They were portrayed as barbarians. What good would it do if we were to be released from one evil pair of hands only to find ourselves thrown into another – even worse than the first captors? However something needed to be done soon; food supplies became scarce and we were only getting one meal a day.

February 10th, midnight; another line-up for another roll-call, this time it was for real – it was obvious we were going to leave. It was dark; people were running all over the place to get to the main square. The Commander and all the guards were present. This was the hour when we were told to get our belongings together and that the march would start in a half hour exactly. Kitchen personnel were ordered to get all food supplies together and load them on hand pulled wagons. No food was to be left in camp – if the sick would have to stay behind with no food supply they would starve to death in case it took too long for someone to come to their rescue and liberate them. And, Hans was one of these people.

It didn't seem too hard to steal some loaves of bread, I thought. The guys carrying bread wrapped in blankets needed both hands... so, unless they were to drop all of the loaves, I figure I had an easy task ahead. I hid in the bushes, and when the next guys passed by I was able to swipe a couple of loaves and brought them straight to the hospital barracks. This went on for a short while (the half-hour to get ready was almost over) and without any problems. Our boys understood what I was doing and did not object at all. Some even slowed down their stride to help me when I was about to grab a loaf or two.

But as it happened so often during my years in concentration camp, there are always those who have to squeal to make themselves look good. And tonight was no exception unfortunately. All of a sudden I was chased by two guards – I was totally unprepared for this. And the moment I pulled my arm back and it came out with a loaf of bread; I was ordered to 'freeze'! Someone grabbed my coat, but I wrestled myself free and started running towards the lavatory – still holding the bread. If it hadn't been such a serious situation, it would have been funny; I was starring in a Keystone Cops movie. I ran through two doors and back through the others – scared to death, but delivering my last loaf safely to the hospital. This had to be it. I could no longer take a chance and risking my life this way. The sick had plenty of bread to survive for a couple days. Hans was still going to try to go with us. He was afraid to stay behind, but in his condition he would not last 'til day's end. So, we managed to convince him to stay – we had a tearful goodbye and went back to start on our dreadful 'Death March' that night.

Roxane Christ

The 'Death March'

CHAPTER VI
The Death March
Either/or...

The first day was a very difficult one. Leaving in the middle of the night, our footfall was the only sound we heard. We were taken through dense forest; the going was rough. We looked like a long line of spooky robot-like creatures marching through the night – one foot in front of the other in an infernal nightmare.

The unusual chore of long-distance walking without prior practice was a torment on everyone's body. It made no difference whether we were well fed or not. I looked around me wondering how long some of the people would be able to cope with this unrelenting punishment on their body and feet. The most unendurable pain was perhaps that you knew where it all began but you didn't know where it would all end. You always knew the beginning – but never the end of the day's march; you had no idea how long you had to travel before you would be allowed to stop.

It did not take long before we had our first casualty. He was a nineteen-year-old boy who was unable to go on after nearly twenty miles. Instead of having mercy on the poor kid and just leave him behind, he was shot to death, together with another guy who was unknown to me. I was selected to dig a grave. One guard was assigned to go with us, armed only of a rifle. We went deep into the forest, carrying the dead bodies and two shovels. This was my chance, I thought. I was going to kill the SS and flee. But what about the other guy – the one assigned to the task with me? Time and time again I was proved that I couldn't rely on a fellow prisoner. With one blow of the shovel I would be able to kill the guard, but if I failed the other guy would probably turn against me in order to save his own skin. A lot of questions ran through my mind at the time. Here was a chance to be free – and no answer came as to whether I should take it. Slowly we began to dig the grave. Not a word was spoken between us. The SS was watching us, his rifle over the shoulder. The hole was deep enough to hold the bodies – it was time to act. The idea of not being able to trust the other guy held me back from killing the guard. And so we took the bodies and rolled them into the grave, covered them with dirt and marched back to the waiting 'marching band'. I would never know what went on in the other guy's mind; I don't even know if he survived the war.

We resumed moving in the direction of Banzlau. This was going to be our first stop. We would rest there for awhile and move on later in the night. When we came in sight of our destination, we stopped abruptly. There was no way we could go to Banzlau – it had been taken over by the Russian army. As a result, we went on walking aimlessly through dense forest all night. The next day we would try and reach Gorlitz. It was daytime now and we were going through familiar places. To the German population we must have been a sight to behold – a long line of striped uniformed prisoners pulling carts with SS passengers aboard going through their city. Lined-up on the sidewalks, they stood there watching us going by as if we were on parade. Knowing and seeing that the end of their oppressive regime was at hand, no one uttered a word; except for a little boy who yelled: "Kill those dirty Jews". It did not faze us. This was something we were used to hearing for years now. But this utterance was followed by an incident we really did not expect to witness and which I would remember forever. The lady standing next to the boy had the courage to slap his face at the moment his mouth closed on the last of his nasty words. A feeling of exultation came over me. Even though no one was able to do anything for us, this show of sympathy carried me a long way during the rest of our journey. *Finally* I had seen some human feelings being displayed where (and at a moment when) I least expected it. In Gorlitz, ironically enough, we were housed at a slaughter house for the night. I guess the Germans needed a rest!

The next day our trip continued through a mountainous area. From 6,000 feet up, we looked down at the city of Swikaw. It was a beautiful sight – everything was quiet and peaceful. Suddenly and without any warning the peace and tranquility of the scene was disrupted; we heard the sound of aircrafts approaching overhead – but we didn't see them. The Germans started running in all directions – panic stricken. This was not the 'Super Breed' Hitler had reared, these people were running scared. Even the guards showed signs of insecurity. And for the first time, they asked us what we would do to them when the war was over! Such a thought should have no place in a super race's mind; instead of being 'fighting machines' they had become 'frightened machines'. But we had to be careful because in an act of desperation they could have killed all of us. Yet, we felt strong now and derived immense satisfaction in telling them that we would take them apart piece by piece when it was all over! I guess they were in shock because none of them reacted.

Every day now four to five prisoners succumbed from sheer exhaustion. They were piled in one of the carts together with the 'near-dead'. We pulled them until we would find a suitable place where to bury them. It was a lugubrious sight – all those bodies piled up on top of one another. Some of them were still moving for hours on end and a lot of them were buried alive. All you did was to close your mind to the sights and sounds. And in all of that misery, we went on following orders 'like sheep to the slaughter'.

Through this ordeal we were still Emil' subjects. Sitting on top of his treasure box aboard one of the cart pulled by two prisoners he was, in spite of everything, a 'privileged person' who did not have to walk all day. He had become meek, maybe realizing that he could soon become one of the people unable to survive the nightmare. The question was; when would King Emil be dethroned?

Our next stop was Regensburg, where food supplies were confiscated at some farms along the way. Then, we continued to err from place to place, never knowing where the end would be. After six weeks of relentless walking between front lines, sleeping in the woods most of the time, we finally arrived at Auschwitz.

Auschwitz was a miserable and frightening place. We entered the camp through the back gate, and we were guided into a big hangar-like building. The place was so crowded that there was hardly anywhere to lie down. Sleeping was only possible if someone would get up and offer his place to you for a short nap. The conditions were unbearable. No lavatories; no fresh water – just one big mess. The gas-chambers had already been put out of commission by the allied bombers, and no one knew what to do with the left-over prisoners.

Prisoners at Auschwitz were usually hauled to 'Canada House' where they would be stripped of all valuables and were told to go 'to the showers' – after which, they would be given back their belongings (mostly jewelry). Often they were then herded to the gas chambers and exterminated without waiting a moment longer.

I am sure the aim had been to exterminate everyone once we had reached Auschwitz but the plan had been thwarted by the allies. Therefore, a new plan had to be put into effect, but none had been elaborated yet. So, for the time being we had to wait for the orders to be handed down from German Headquarters.

One night one man approached me and asked some of us if we wanted to play cards – why not? So, we started playing…

Meanwhile conditions did not get better; people dropped dead in front of our eyes almost on every hour of the day.

As it happens, in the middle of the card game someone near us dropped dead… We simply turned him over and continued playing using his body as a card-table!

Although we were there for four days only, and no one cared to even look at us, many people lost their last hope of surviving and died of despair. As for food, I can't remember if we even ate during that time – nor do I remember being hungry.

On the third day at around 10:00pm, a roll-call was called via a public address system asking all prisoners to assemble in the main square. Stepping outside of the hangar we could see the guards in the towers – machine guns aimed at the center of the square. Flood-lights made the night look like daytime. Strangely enough, not a soul followed the Commander's order. Even the second call showed no result. The main reason for this overt disobedience was the frightening thought of being executed by the firing squad standing at the ready in the towers at the four corners of the square. Thus, everyone stayed inside the hangar. This was not a show of solidarity – but simple individual terror. Our disobedience did not engender any punitive action by the SS, and we were left alone for the rest of the night. Floodlights were dimmed and quiet and relative peace fell on the camp once again. When the dawn came however, the roll-call was renewed. It did not look as grim as the night before – now we could see what was going on. The daylight helped to get us out of the hangar and into the main square. Like a flock of sheep we took our positions. The machine guns were aimed at us once again, yet it didn't look as frightening as it did at ten o'clock the previous night. But, we were still unsure of the fate awaiting us.

As for me, I had decided to rush the fence at the first sound of shooting; close to the fence I would be safe from gunfire, and I would play dead and wait – hopeful not to be noticed.

Minutes seemed to stretch into hours. Finally the Commander announced that we were going to be split into divisions of fifteen hundred men; our destination would be another 'bad' concentration camp – Dachau.

In view of the overcrowded conditions existing in Dachau already, each division was allowed to arrive at the site with only two hundred and fifty prisoners. Nobody told us what would happen to the remaining twelve hundred and fifty men in each division – that were not supposed to reach Dachau; we were soon to find out the answer to that question.

Roxane Christ

The prisoners' barracks at Dachau

Now, survival became a day-to-day proposition, and I am sure if we had known help was near at hand, most of us would have fled in hope of being rescued or in panic of being killed on the spot. The next eight weeks would be the most dismal experience I would ever live, and which I would never forget. Our first stop was to be a camp by the name of Flossenberg. It was not a matter of distance any more; it was just a matter of knowing where the day would end to be able to rest our tired bones.

On this stretch of our journey, a black and white fox terrier, which was probably looking for company followed us on our trek. We became attached to him, and even shared what little food we had, with him. But we soon realized that the Polish prisoners had their eye on the little pooch and mentioned to us that dog meat would make a very tasty meal! From that moment on, we kept a close eye on our little friend so that no harm would come to him. However, in a moment of

120

distraction, the dog was lured away from our group and before we had a chance to come to his aid, his head was brutally smashed in; we were stunned and powerless. How could someone be so low as to kill a poor little helpless creature? Here was an animal that trusted us and gave us so much affection, and which in return, was brutally slaughtered. Even though we were as hungry as the rest, the thought of killing the dog would never have crossed our mind.

Flossenberg was somewhat of a relief – it was more like an army camp than a concentration camp. The food was good, the sleeping quarters clean and we were told that we were needed to stay for the time it would take us to build a fence around the camp – it wasn't even fenced in! We had found a haven amid the madness…

With the allied forces being so close, we tried to postpone death as long as possible. Every sunrise, every sunset could mean the end for us. But after going on for so long, no one dared to talk about 'Liberation Day' – perhaps because of the order the Germans had received to shoot fifty prisoners a day. They were picked at random but in an organized fashion and from the back of the procession. One way to beat this system was to take a short cut whenever the hoard would go round a corner. If you ended up at the back of the pack after the morning's line-up you needed to make sure to get to the front of the procession in a hurry otherwise this could be your last day on earth. Lucky for the ones who really made an effort to survive; their chances became greater because of the apathy shown by the rest of the fellows who had already given up on life.

When you were in a state of depression, you did not care about the future anymore; all you wanted to do was to end it right there and then. Everybody had days like that. So, one morning during the march, it was my turn to feel that there were no more reasons to go on living. Depressed as I was then, I decided that this was it – that day I was going to end it. I stayed at the back of the pack and figured this was as good a day as any to die. I even made sure I was the last man in the procession. I was relaxed and enjoyed myself at admiring the scenery. The two SS officers walking behind me seemed to take pleasure in teasing me. My pants were torn to shreds in the crotch, and they tried to tear them ever more by putting a stick between my legs. It did not disturb me in the least; this was to be their last chance to make the rest of my life a misery.

All of a sudden there was a lot of commotion ahead of the pack. For the first and the last time fifty guys were picked *from the front* of the procession! They were shot and left behind without being buried. Actually I didn't really feel bad at not succeeding in my plan to end my days – this incident lifted my spirit and gave me the courage to continue fighting for my life, or mere survival.

Roaming the countryside for days on end we soon realized that we were returning to Flossenberg. But once we came in sight of our piece of 'heaven' we were told to turn around once again – the Russians were already occupying the town. Consequently, we went on walking aimlessly through the forest trying to find a shelter away from the firing lines. The Germans told us all kinds of stories about the barbaric Russians and all of the crimes they committed against the civilian population. Apparently, stealing and raping were everyday occurrences; they were seen wearing watches on both arms from shoulders to wrists. This type of coaxing affected us so much that we became more afraid of the Russians than we were of the Germans. All we could hope for at that point in time was to encounter some English or American forces.

Our circumstances were most wretched now. Sometimes we had to do without food for several days. When we had nothing else to eat we ate grass in a desperate attempt to fill our stomach – not realizing that our digestive system was not designed to handle this type of herbivore feeding. The result of the adoption of such an emergency diet was soon to be felt by way of the worst abdominal cramps and bloody diarrhea, which would kill all of us in no time at all. Seeing (and mostly feeling) the outcome of ingesting grass, I decided that I would rather die hungry than on a full stomach but in terrible pain.

Walking long distances in the forest, going from nowhere to nowhere, became a way of life for us; nights turned into days and the days into nights with hardly any rest. This nightmare worked on the SS state of mind as well. They became unsure of their future and made desperate moves – every day more and more of them disappeared, leaving only very few guards to watch over us. Those were the fanatics who still believed in their chance to turn the tide, and they would not give us an opportunity to be taken by the allied forces.

One day when we just finished a short rest, one of them walked up to me and put his gun to my head. "Run," he said, prodding me with the gun. I knew that if I ran he would shoot me and have the excuse that he killed a fleeing prisoner. If he really wanted to kill me, he had to do it now and I was not going to give him the excuse for pulling the trigger. I held my position and told him that if he wanted to shoot me he would have to do it right there and then. I was not going to move an inch. There was absolutely no bravery on my part; I took it for granted that I was going to be shot anyhow – but not the way they planned it at that minute. If he would have done it a few days ago when I was in the throws of depression, I surely would have obliged, but now I was more determined than ever to survive.

Walking day and night took its toll. The Germans took their rest sitting aboard the carts that we pulled. We, on the other hand, depended on their good will to rest. But we learned the art of sleeping while we walked. We walked five across in a row. The person in the center would put his arms around the people next to him – they would support his weight during the time he slept. After a while we would trade places so the next guy could take a nap. It was an eerie sight, but this was the only way to get some sleep.

Once in a while we stopped at a farm, and the farmer was ordered to come up with a meal for us! Generally the farmer was unfamiliar with the amount of food to be cooked all at once for so many mouths to feed. Of course, the last in line would be left hungry most of the time. The message would spread like wild fire through the lines when the farmer was about to run out of food. The stronger ones bullied their way to the front, to get some precious life-saving food; the rest of us struggled... Sometimes it was better to forget about food on that day and take a chance on the following day to get some raw vegetables or potatoes out of the fields we passed. If we did not wander off too far and stayed in sight of the guards we were able to get into the fields to relieve ourselves, as long as we returned within minutes. Throughout the years of incarceration and working in nearby fields, we were able to distinguish crops like agricultural experts. So, as we were walking along the countryside, we would wait for the right moment (or the right field to appear in sight), rush down to the most favorable spot, pull our pants down, beside a beet, or a potato patch and grope around to swipe some of the produce and bring it back without being punished.

To push your way to the front of the line to get some food was dangerous if not deadly. One morning we were lined up in front of a farmhouse when someone spread the word that the farmer was running low in provision; I made a dash for it. Next to me another fellow prisoner, unknown to me, took off at the same time as I did. An officer yelled at us to go back into the line, but there was no way to stop us now. We would be picked out and punished anyhow, so we went on running. If I had realized the severity of our decision, I would not have taken a chance at all. The officer drew his pistol and aimed. I heard the whistle of the bullet.

In an instant I looked back and saw the other fellow lying on the ground – a bullet hole in the middle of his forehead. He was not bleeding and he was not moving; he looked as if he was asleep. It did not penetrate my brain that he was dead; and went to the front of the line – and got a meal that day! After the incident sank in and I finally realized that I could have been the one shot dead for wanting to eat, I promised myself never to run a risk like that again.

In those days at the end of the war, it seemed the Germans took out their frustration on us and would do anything to tear us apart. At one time, when we stopped at another farm where we were going to bed down for the night, we had to wait standing on the road for arrangements to be made. This was a small country road with a bubbling creek running on both sides of the road. A couple of SS guards who wanted to have some fun were pushing the back of the pack forward by yelling at their German Shepherd dogs to 'fetch us'. The mean, barking dogs showed their teeth – ready to attack at any show of dissention among us. No wonder we panicked. But there was nowhere to go. However the joke backfired. One of the dogs got so scared that he turned around and attacked his handler, biting off his nose… The dog was shot on the spot, but the handler became the victim of his own trick – he died from his injuries the same day.

When we were led inside the farm, straw was spread all over the stable and a good night sleep seemed to be a promise – but it wasn't to be. Once everyone had settled down something; an allied forces' bomb crashed through the roof and took most of it off… The ripped half of the roof uncovered a star-filled sky. We were lucky that the incident didn't end up in a firing blaze. In the end we went to sleep as if nothing had happened.

During the night however, many of us thought of escaping but we were still unsure of our surroundings, very few tried – I don't know if they made it. And this sense of insecurity was somewhat enhanced when one day while crossing the Oder River, a prisoner had the courage to take the bold step of jumping over the railing of the bridge into the churning water. Everyone rushed to the railing to watch his escape. We all hoped he would succeed. He was swept away swiftly, but it did not take long for the Germans to begin their target shooting. We cheered at every bullet that missed its aim. If we would have known what lousy shots they were, many more would have tried to escape on that morning. But all of a sudden luck ran out for the escapee; his coat opened up, making him a bigger target. We saw the water turn red around him; we knew he had been hit. He went down, whether he did it on purpose or not we would never know. For my part I hope he survived the ordeal. He deserved to live if only for his courage.

After weeks of trudging we still had not reached our destination. It seemed that we were going nowhere, still going from forest to forest trying to hide from public view and from the allied forces. But we did not always succeed. It was a cold day in February, while we were aimlessly trekking through the woods when a British fighter plane was heard and seen flying low overhead. He nearly touched the tree-tops. If he

127

could fly that low without being shot down; that meant the Allied Forces were not far off from our position. Maybe he discovered us and would call in the troops to rescue us out of our tormentor's grip. Wouldn't that be terrific? And it seemed that my silent wish was to be granted. The plane took a second run over our heads; even flying lower now.

WW II British Spitfire

A staccato of bullets aimed at our pack whistled through the trees and fifty or more prisoners fell to death at the hands of our own allies! The Germans were all saved. They had hit the ground the moment they had heard the plane – their guns trained at us, they used us as a shield to protect themselves. Why were we shot at? I don't know. We were clearly visible and recognizable in our striped uniforms – we looked more like zebras than soldiers. And the Germans got their daily quota of slaughtered prisoners without firing a single shot.

Up until now I had survived pretty well without any bodily harm – that would leave any visible marks; apart from an occasional beating but that was all. Lady luck seemed to have kept me company up to that point, but I was not to come out unscathed.

Very near exhaustion all the time, you could not help but doze off once in a while at roll-call, and it was customary when you accidentally missed calling off your number somebody next to you would take charge and either call off your number for you or wake you up before your number was up. Not today however! The count had gone wrong several times, and the officer taking it was losing his patience. The next count went wrong again… This time I missed to call out my number. The officer became so mad that he hit my face with the butt of his gun – repeatedly.

I tried to protect my face as much as possible, but the damage was done. I had a deep cut in my cheek, and all of my teeth were either broken or knocked out. I did not even dare to spit them out until it was all over. When he calmed down, he left me lying on the ground. My fellow prisoners helped me to my feet; my head felt as if it had blown to twice its normal size. For days after that, I felt miserable, but the end was near and I would take my revenge somehow. As a result, I had to soak my food in water because I could not chew it, but yet I had to eat whenever I had the chance. Food was not always available – actually there were more days without food than days when we found a farmer willing to feed us. And even if the man was unable or uncooperative everything he had was confiscated and taken with us to continue on our journey. On one occasion we thought we had it made… The farm at which we stopped was thoroughly searched and we found sides of pork meat. We cooked them on an open fire and feasted upon them until we could not eat anymore. However, this exceptional meal worked against us. Most of us weighed between sixty and eighty pounds and had not eaten rich food for years. Eating that fatty meat made us sick – that's all we needed! Not the Germans though; they feasted for days.

Often we went from feast to famine, and we stooped so low as to ask our captors for some bread crumbs – literally. They would throw them on the ground and would get their kicks at seeing the scrambling bodies fighting over pieces of bread. As if this wasn't enough to satisfy their thirst for humiliating us, their new game was to wait until they would find a pile of horse shit and put a piece of bread in the center to see how far we would go to get our feed. The first time I saw them doing it, I was astonished – although nothing should have surprised me at this point. And I did not believe my eyes when I saw some of the prisoners debasing themselves to the point of fetching the bread amid the manure in such a humiliating way. I would have died rather than getting a crumb out from a pile of shit. I guess I still had some pride in me that would not have allowed me to stoop down to that level. The so-called 'Aryan Race' had triumphed again – but for me they were the *scum* of the Human Race. We could only hope the tide would turn soon.

These SS scum were real cowards at heart. This was confirmed during a confrontation they had with the regular army on a railroad emplacement. Upon crossing the railroad we found a battalion of German soldiers waiting for us. As customary, we begged them for some food. Seeing the condition we were in, they sympathized with us and brought us some food – against the wishes of our Commander. He ordered us to return the food and started to beat us pitilessly. The army officer demanded to know what we had done to be so severely beaten. The SS replied that he should mind his own business and to shut up. The army officer drew his gun and demanded that the SS stopped the beating at once. Everyone stood bated breath waiting for the result of this altercation. It was a stand-off for a few minutes. Guns were drawn on both sides; and we were in the middle! Finally the SS backed down. I am sure they did not want to risk a fire fight. This showed us that there were still some Germans who cared what happened to us.

Matcek would show us how important the struggled for surviving could be. (He was the one Emil punished by hanging.) On that day we had walked about thirty miles when we arrived at another farm. It was a long time since we had a night's sleep under a roof, so we were glad to get to somewhere that could house us and give us some bedding on which to rest our tired body. There was even a chance we would get a decent meal. Since there were only four hundred men left we would have a better chance to get a share, and with only a hundred and fifty left to be killed, there was yet a better chance at survival.

Someone found a huge pile of grain in the attic, and word spread around quickly. Before I went to sleep I made up my mind to get my share, but I decided to wait until dawn to make my move. So, early the next morning I was ready to give it a try. Most people were still asleep, and a lot of them were too weak to get up to the attic anyway. I thought I was the first one to try my luck. I knew that if I succeeded the others would follow. The only way to the attic was via a pole. This presented no problem. I climbed the pole with practically no effort (there was no fat left on me to hinder my climb). To my surprise Matcek was already there. I assumed he was there for the same reason as mine. I knelt down and was filling my cap with grains when I felt a chocking grip on the nape of my neck. I was powerless to move and being on my knees my assailant had the advantage over me. I could not believe my ears when I heard Matcek call for help in order to turn me in... The guard came up to his help and ordered me to put the grain back and to come down. Since I knew that I was going to get a beating, I filled my cap again in the same move that had emptied it moments earlier and put it back on my head. I slid down the pole, expecting to be beaten, but not anticipating for it to be as hard as it was – it was unbelievable. Blows from left, right landed on every part of my body. Some of the blows were cushioned by the grain hidden in my cap. I started bleeding from my ears but kept my cool – somehow... "Officer," I screamed, "why only me? What about the other guys up there. There are more up there!" The moment he looked up to confirm my lie; I was gone – crawling away between other prisoners, hiding my head under a blanket. He rushed up to me but not recognizing me he asked where did that guy go? I answered: "You mean the one you hit just now?"

"Yes," he snarled.

"Oh, he went to the back," I replied. And off he went in search of his prey. In the meantime our morning roll-call was called. With the help of a friend I got to the line-up. They helped me stand up. The beating had taken its toll on me. I fainted, which meant that if I didn't come out of it before the count ended, I would be shot and left behind. I had tried not to pass out but I had not succeeded. However, Lady Luck made a come back. The count was incorrect; someone was missing. The second count did nothing to change the result – someone had fled the scene. This was an insult to them; and...another count was taken. I don't know how the third count ended but I know that at least it gave me a chance to recover fully. I don't know how long I was unconscious, but I was the hero in the eyes of my friends – only because their efforts to keep me alive had succeeded. And believe me; I was glad to share my trove of grain with them. This episode showed me once again, that only a handful of individuals could be trusted in dire situations.

With the allies being so close, we would make every effort *not* to reach Dachau. It made no sense to take a chance in another extermination camp. We figured that it should be possible amid the existing chaos, to find somebody who would be willing to help us if we escaped. So, Max, Lou and I put our heads together and planned our escape to freedom. We had been together through all those years, but now it would be better to go one at a time. Straws were drawn to decide who would flee first. Max was the first one to go.

Our plan was straightforward; the next time we would go into a forest, Lou and I would start a fight, Max would flee while the guards would be distracted by the commotion. He would go downhill, and even if he lost his footing he would continue downhill. Trees would give him a natural protection. Our plan worked to perfection. When the shooting began, it was too late; Max was out of reach already. What happened to him will remain a mystery. All I know is that he did not return! There were only the two of us left now. We would wait a couple of days before we would try the next escape. Lou would be next. The Germans became sloppy and disorganized in their duty to guard us. There were only a few guards actually, and the guard-dogs had been retired a long time ago. But the few SS left continued to take their frustration out on us in these last few weeks of the war. I would even go as far as saying that they redoubled their efforts to be cruel.

Throughout the journey Emil had taken advantage of his knowledge and familiarity with the countryside. For him it was easy to disappear in the crowd; he wore civilian clothes and spoke the language like one born in the land. And one morning he did – disappear that is. Andries, who had stayed with Emil since he had first joined him, was left on his own now. So, out of the clan of five Dutchmen there were still three of us left, plus Erwin Backenroth whom we counted as one of us.

The end of the war was in sight, and if we survived it would be only because of the way we helped each other. I was a strong-headed man, but one who had counted on the moral support of my friends more than once. They were the thinkers, I was the impulsive doer.

I remember while we were still at camp, on a day like any other day, since they had nothing eise to do, the SS set a barrack on fire just for kicks, with about a hundred people inside – I followed my impulse and rushed inside the burning building. Amongst the people inside, there was no panic – only apathy; which made it easy for me to get a bunch of prisoners out on the first run. I told them to form a chain by holding hands and that I would get them out... The first group came out with no problem at all – applauded by everybody watching the spectacle (including the Germans). But I was still blinded by utter rage, and ran back to get the rest of the prisoners out of the inferno. In my rush, I didn't even realize that someone had had enough brains to douse me with water before I ran in the burning barrack for the second time. Meanwhile some of the prisoners had smashed windows and got out of their own accord. Everyone came out safely after the second run. No one was really hurt and the only remnants of that incident were smoke inhalation for some of us and a scorched eye brow for me. Everyone hailed me as their hero, but, believe me, hero's don't exist – only a fool would do a thing like that on impulse, because the moment you give yourself a chance to think things through, you would never take such a risk. The extra piece of bread I got as a reward couldn't be compared to the satisfaction I drew out of the experience.

Lou Emmerik was my best advisor and supporter during our days in concentration camp, and even though my escape was not due to occur for a few days yet, we worked out a plan of action that I would have to follow to the letter if I wanted to be free at long last. Since Max' successful escape and because the Germans knew of our friendship, we were watched closely with suspicious looks following us everywhere. I guess they wanted to take revenge for the way we conned them into letting Max escape. But before mine, it was Lou's turn to escape.

Neither of our plans worked out in the end. Lou became very weak and sick and he felt if he continued walking it would be the end for him – but if he stayed behind, he would be shot; our plans had to be changed. Instead of just giving up, he agreed to wait until we found a place to hide, which would give him at least a chance at survival. We had been walking along a road with a lot of hiding places for several hours. All we had to do now was to wait for the order to stop and rest. Houses were visible at a distance. With some houses still in sight we finally stopped to rest. Lou and I disappeared in the underbrush in quest of a place for him to hide. It did not take us long to find a gully just wide enough to hold his body comfortably. We decided that he should lie down to take a nap and after a while he could go and check if anyone in these houses would be willing to help him. We knew the risks involved, but he had already chosen to die; at worst, he would do so in a humane way. I covered the gully with branches and foliage until no one could guess there was someone hidden beneath the brush. After getting a satisfying answer from him that he was comfortable, I left him hoping that I would see him soon. Whether he slept and died in his sleep or whether he made it to town, I will never know. Although I am quite sure he did not survive.

A couple days later we stopped on another country road. The only friends I had left were Andries and Erwin. I had given up on my plans to escape. I decided to try and hold out as long as I could and wait for the end result. I was totally emaciated. My weight was down to a mere sixty pounds. How long could I continue to struggle to remain alive before I had to stop fighting and lie down to die? All of these thoughts ran through my head whilst standing on this lonely country road. There were only twenty guards to watch over us. All of a sudden they hit the ground like they had done once before. The only thing that flashed before my eyes then was the sight of those men that died during the British air raid. This time however, the guards didn't order us to stand where we were – we hoped not to be shot down again. After a few minutes of unbearable anticipation; nothing happened. And we resumed walking. Erwin was near the end of his strength as well. He talked to me about giving up on life. Since I was over my depression I tried to talk him out of quitting. He turned down everyone of my arguments in favor of living and of fighting. There was no way of moving him. I don't know whether

I had a premonition or if I said what I said out of sheer desperation, but I uttered words I could even contemplate being true myself. "Erwin, don't be such a fool. This is our Liberation Day. Today we are going to be freed."

To him however, it was just another way to try convincing him not to give up, – and, he stubbornly refused to listen, sat down and was promptly shot to death! A half-hour later we were liberated… His brutal murder carried out by people devoid of human feelings had been for naught. And no one will ever convince me that the guard who executed him didn't do so out of resentment and to settle a personal grudge for losing the war.

As I said, a half-hour after Erwin died needlessly, we stopped again in front of a gate on the side of another country road. The guards were gone now. It was quiet around us. A feeling of apprehension invaded me – 'something is wrong,' I thought. Why were we standing here? This eerie silence could only mean one thing for all of us – *death*. The iron-gate was opened on us by an old man in uniform who invited us inside the camp and closed the gate behind us. Somehow we had arrived to our final destination – Lebanau. We all went to the barracks without being asked to do so. We did that instinctively I suppose – a barrack meant protection. There was a fire burning inside which was a welcomed feeling and sight. The long awaited news came to us without drum roll or flag waving or parades but we knew it was true; we were told that our misery had come to an end – *the war was over…*

The first thing I did was to undress, stand naked near the fire and burn my lice-ridden clothes. I was neither glad, nor happy – we all had suffered too much. It did not even register that I was a free man again. For nearly three years I had been ordered around, and suddenly I was free to make my own decision, to act as I pleased, to be my own man again... I didn't know what that meant anymore. It was going to be hard to return to civilian life. But for now all I wanted to do was to sleep – for a long, long time. Just then, the door of the barrack was flung opened by a six-foot G.I. This mountain of a black man entered the room holding up in the air the biggest present ever to be given to someone who had been incarcerated in a concentration camp for so long – a real live SS man! He looked small in more ways than one; dangling there in the G.I.'s hands screaming that he wasn't an SS man... This was easy to check. They had a mark in their armpit identifying them as SS members. He was put down in the middle of the barrack floor. The G.I. left, closing the door behind him. Now we had an SS enemy all to ourselves. *His* life depended on *us* – ours had depended on his for far too long; the tables were turned. He was the one who was scared now. First we checked his SS brand to make certain there wasn't any mistake – sure enough he had been one of our tormentors. Cowardly, he begged for his life; his SS bravado was gone, he tried to convince us that he had not harmed any of us personally. It was time for us to show some mercy... but that was impossible...

Only a few of us were strong enough to participate in our freedom celebration. All of the terrible things they had done to us came back to mind. I will not describe how we punished him sufficed to say that we were guided by blind hatred – we simply took him apart, piece by piece; he finally died twenty minutes later. We had seen and severed every part of his human body.

When it was all over, instead of being satisfied and my vengeance satiated through our deed, I sat down and cried like a child; anger turned into aversion, so that when the second SS was brought in, I could not bring myself to participate in his execution. This one died of fright; being thrown in the middle of us without any escape route had been too much for him to bear.

CHAPTER VII
Aftermath

Freedom – The New Fear

The following day the American forces moved in and took charge of the camp, and I became a link between the Americans and the prisoners because I was one of the few people who could communicate with both. Most of the prisoners spoke either German or their own language, and so did the Americans.

Their first task was to keep us alive – now that we had survived they needed to get us back to *life*. Many of us had physical problems which were an aftermath of our concentration camp years. Thus, after a while the camp looked like a hospital – nurses and doctors were running in all directions looking after too many patients. The nurses were Germans, and they really did everything they could to ease our pain.

We were all taken to a bathhouse, bathed by nurses and sprayed with DDT, which freed us from lice for the first time since I don't know when.

One thing they soon discovered was that their loving care could kill us! Being hungry over such a long period of time made us eat whatever was presented to us – and then some. We were still mentally afraid not to have enough the next day. What's more, our stomachs responded very badly to pork meat. I think they over-fed us out of sympathy and to get our weight to viable level once again. However, many of us reacted to the remedy to our suffering. We were soon plagued with diseases that would kill the lot of us even though the war was over! TB and Typhoid fever were as common as colds and with an average of sixty pounds; our bodies had taken all of the beatings they could stand.

As for me, it didn't take long until I felt that something was wrong. I was feverish and tried to hide it, because I thought an interpreter was irreplaceable… A few days later I collapsed and I was put in the hospital and found out they could manage very well without me. I needed them more than they needed me. The diagnosis was typhoid fever; I had another fight ahead of me.

I didn't want to die now that the war was over. If I gave up now I would let everyone down who had believed in my return – therefore I wanted to prove that a sixty pound body still had some fighting left in it. If my body could hold on, my mental state would pull me through. And even though my stomach refused food, I kept on eating stubbornly. However when my sight abandoned me, I was ready to throw in the towel, I was ready to die. I did not want to go through life blind after having conquered all of the other problems that I had faced during my incarceration. I didn't want people to look at me with sympathy and say: "Look how that poor guy survived the war…" NO! If I could not regain my sight, I would not be able to cope with everyday life. So, I asked the doctor to stop the treatment immediately. But he was so convinced that my 'temporary blindness' (as he called it) was part of the typhoid symptomatic process and that it would disappear after a while, that he convinced me… And I decided to give him my undivided confidence and to keep on fighting.

I could only recognize people's voices now and I was not aware of my surroundings. I could only guess at what went on around me. Everything was black; day and night was the same. The only difference was that daytime was noisier. On the other hand the silence in the middle of the night would grip me with uncontrollable fear. I felt I was going to die – for the first time in my life I panicked. I screamed for help; I knew there was a button somewhere that would alarm the nurse. I groped around me while I continued screaming thereby creating a lot of commotion. Finally I succeeded in alerting the staff. All of a sudden I was surrounded by a lot of people. I heard them talk about a crisis, but did not know what that meant. A priest was called in to give the last rites; he put something on my tongue and I heard him pray. I also felt a needle penetrating my leg. Creeping warmth rose through my entire body. I calmed down with a sense of reassurance that I was in good hands and fell asleep.

I don't know who did the job – the priest or the doctor, but the next day I felt a lot better. I was still blind, but I was confident in the doctor's assurance that it would soon pass.

One of my everyday visitors was Andries, who survived the ordeal unscathed. I don't know what came over me one day, but when Andries expressed his desire to smoke some American cigarettes, instead of telling him to go and ask a G.I. for it, I described exactly the location where he could find a stash of cigarettes. The place was a building three blocks from where I was and which I had never seen before. Yet, I was able to describe all of the rooms inside the building and I had a picture in my mind of a boarded-up basement containing the cigarettes. I guess I had experienced some sort of extra-sensory perception, because Andries came back with the cigarettes. He had found them exactly where I had told him they would be. He was astonished by the accuracy of my directions. All I said in a matter-of-fact tone of voice: "I told you so!"

My hospital stay was a long and pleasant one. The immobility and the good food lifted my weight quickly to a healthy 140 pounds, but the gain had been far too quick… My legs could not support my weight anymore – I had to learn to walk again. This was made especially difficult since I had not regained my sight yet and I felt very insecure. But soon there were indications that blindness was dissipating – slowly I began to see shadows passing by my bed; I knew I was on my way to a full recovery.

Only one big problem remained. My years in confinement made me shy of the outside world. And whatever the staff tried, to lure me into taking a stroll outside the barrack, it failed. Help came however in the form of a terrible earache. The doctor was called in and he told me that there was no way for him to treat me unless I came to his office across the way; and added that if I wanted to come to see him there, he would be in his office for me at any time during the day. Since I had regained my sight by this time, I had no excuses not to visit him. What's more, my shyness created no sympathy in the other guys. Being left alone to resolve this dilemma, still in pain my only recourse to end the suffering was to cross the yard and visit the doctor in his office. The next day I worked up enough courage to do just that – the pain had not abated during the night, as I had hoped. When I reached his office, I discovered that it had been all a hoax to get me out of the hospital. All the doctor did was to put some drops in my ear and send me on my way. Standing outside of the barrack I felt the sun warming my body – it was a beautiful spring morning. I started walking around a little enjoying my newly regained freedom. Then I walked some more… I walked on for hours – so much so that I didn't want to go back inside… Finally I got a taste of *freedom*. It was late that night when I decided to return to the hospital… I had taken another step on the road of recovery; I felt relieved.

My total recovery from typhoid took some six weeks. Yet my behavior was not normal. Sometimes I did the craziest things. One day we left camp; down the road there was a farm house and to me this meant food, which was still an obsession with us – even though food was now plentiful. And, I went to see the farmer and asked him to give me one chicken. He refused! The next thing I know, I am shooting the chicken I wanted and taking it back to camp. There, the people had no idea what to do with the fowl so I handed it to the kitchen personnel, they took it in good grace and I never saw the chicken again. How did I come in possession of a gun, you ask? I don't remember. Whether I stole it or it was given to me, or found on the German uniform that I was wearing – to this day it is still a mystery to me.

We were an odd bunch, all of us wearing a Nazi uniform. Thus, it was no surprise to me that one day when we went to town and I wandered off from the group no one made any effort to stop us on our strange escapade. On that occasion I entered private homes and offices looking at all the things I had not seen in a long time. Nobody asked any questions or tried to throw me out. Maybe this was the aftermath of the war or perhaps people were still afraid of their own men in uniform. If they would have asked what I was doing, I wouldn't have been able to give them an answer. When I entered a clothing store and told the owner to show me some nice suits he obliged and fitted me with two suits of prime quality – I walked out with 'my purchase' without paying for it. It had not sunk in yet that I had to pay for whatever I wanted with money again. However, the proprietor did nothing to stop me. While I was on my shopping spree, the boys were looking all over the place trying to find me. When they found me – purely by accident it was time to go 'home' to camp. But I was two suits richer than when I left it. I never wore the suits, because when the time came for me to return to Holland, I left the suits behind feeling more secure wearing the Nazi uniforms than civil clothes – These Nazi uniforms for which I had had to show respect for all those years.

It was the second week of July, and most people had forgotten the elation of all of the prisoners returning to their homeland… The first leg of the journey was accomplished aboard an American army truck. It seemed that the G.I. who was driving the truck was trying to set a land-speed record. He hustled us around at every corner he took until he finally sideswiped a tree! We were thrown clear off the truck – most of us were slightly injured. The driver checked for damages on his vehicle and it wasn't bad enough for us not to continue on the journey. I got off lightly from this incident with a broken bone in one of my feet. When we recovered enough we got back into the truck and went on our way to our first destination – Strasburg. There I was treated by a doctor who bandaged my foot tightly enabling me to hobble along and until I could get better help in my country. In my German boots, which were about a size too big, I had enough support for my damaged foot to carry me through. From Strasburg we went homeward via Paris, where we stayed at the Dutch Consulate on the Champs Elysée. We were in Paris for only four days – to discover that a lot of people had not learned anything from the war! Being free now, I didn't expect a 'royal welcome' but at least some decent food. So, when my first meal consisted of a chunk of bread and, believe it or not, a 'plate' of black coffee, I decided to put in a complaint with the Dutch Ambassador. An audience was granted but the man told me in the sternest of fashion that if I didn't like the way I was treated I could go back to the concentration camp!

In Auschwitz we had a doctor who was nicknamed 'The Hangman of Auschwitz' because of all the murders he had committed while experimenting with all sorts of drugs on the prisoners. Most of the experiments had deadly results. I had never met the man, so it was a surprise to me when some of the guys on our transport discovered that 'The Hangman' had had the guts, after hiding for awhile, to come out and try to escape punishment by posing as a prisoner himself. If, this had occurred a couple of months earlier we would have killed him outright. But in this instance we decided to hand him over to the Dutch Ambassador. We led him to his office and waited patiently to see what would happen to 'our prisoner'. Although we waited for a long time, we did not see him or the Ambassador anymore; neither did we get an answer as to 'The Hangman's' whereabouts. I suspect that he was returned to freedom after having a 'friendly chat' with the Ambassador. This would be in line with the Ambassador's stand against me when I complained. I never read in any newspapers of the capture of the Auschwitz executioner and I am sorry I didn't report the fact to our government for further investigation at the time – but this is all water under the bridge now...

Four days were gone, and we were on our way to our final destination – Amsterdam, Holland. But first, we had to stop off in Eidhoven Fillips Electronic Factory. There I was informed that Hans, who had stayed behind in Kittlitzstreben, had been liberated only two days after our departure on our horrible 'Death March' and that he was now in England with the English Forces. I wrote him a card telling him of the fate of our friends. Three of us had survived; Hans, Andries and me. But *who were the lucky ones?* I don't rightly know. The road ahead would be rough, particularly in view of the fact that assistance for the Holocaust survivors was non-existent.

It was time now to prepare myself for the reunion with my family and friends in Amsterdam. I did not expect a welcome committee, but the reception I received was no better than a cold shower. Nobody was there to help me. A couple of desks in the basement of the railroad station indicated that the basement was used as 'an office' assigned to provide aid to the returning prisoners. I decided just to stop somebody and ask for help. It took a while for me to find someone who knew anything about the job! At least the person told me to sit down and not to go straight home! I was given an address where I was told I could stay for the night and in case they wanted to get in touch with me. They also told me that they would first phone my family. This sounded strange to me because we never had a phone, but, I thought, maybe they had gotten one right after the war. So, I waited, and waited – alone in that basement. I felt as though no one cared about me. Tired of waiting, I suppose, I decided to take some action of my own. I found the person and told him that I had been patient long enough and demanded to know why he had me waiting for all that time. He simply told me that he had completely forgotten about me... He also told me that since his call to my family had been left unanswered, he didn't think it was important to find out why that was so. After questioning him as to who he really called, it turned out that he had contacted the fire department across the street! The reason for doing so was that they wanted to confirm that my family was still living at the given address; they phoned the fire department to ask them if the house was still standing.

The circle was now complete. I left the same station as the one I left when it all started. I left as a prisoner of the Germans and I returned as a prisoner of my own insecurity. I did not know where to begin my new life. I stepped out of the station prudently. Everything outside looked the same as I had left it. I wanted to scream: "Hey guys, don't you see me? I am back!" But no one noticed me or paid attention to me, even though I was still wearing a Nazi uniform! The fact that I was back did not concern any one at all... I felt a stranger in my own hometown.

Amsterdam

I was afraid to go home, and in order to postpone my confrontation with reality as much as possible, I took the long way home, walking instead of taking a streetcar. But even if I would have liked to use public transport, I couldn't have done so – I was still penniless. As a result, I walked, thinking about what I would say to my parents, and how they would react to my returning home. One more block to go, and around the corner would be my house. I turned the corner – all of the houses were the same as when I left three years ago except for our house and the one next door to it. They were both razed to the ground… I stared, and stared at this empty space where my home used to be; there was nothing left but emptiness. There was emptiness in my mind as well.

I decided to sit back and see how I was going to handle this situation. First I went to the address I had been given at the railroad station. It turned out to be an old diamond factory in Albert Cuyp Street where many more of my companions were already living in temporary housing. I was taken in 'as one of them' and given a small amount of money; said to be an allowance, handed a change of clothes and was told that for the time being to do as I pleased. So, I was now 'housed' with other repatriated people who had lived and survived through similar experiences as me and who were confronted with solving the same problems – to try and fit into 'civilian society' once again. Everyone went about resolving this issue in a different manner.

For my part I looked round for people I once knew but all I saw were strangers. Uncle Jan's bar was still standing at the corner... Maybe he could give me a clue about what happened to my parents?

I entered the bar, and Uncle Jan asked me what he could do for me – he hadn't recognized me. I *re-introduced myself* to him and he finally told me what happened to my family. My father had indeed returned from Westerbork as promised but the whole family was re-captured in November 1943 to be sent to concentration camps in Germany. My head was spinning – I didn't know what to do; commit suicide? Drowning myself would be the easy way out! But – Did I go through three years of hardship to kill myself now? NO!

It was strange how you try to go back to the old routine. The first thing I did was to see whether the old clothing factory was there and who came back. Mijntje, my former girlfriend still lived at the same address, I was told – and I went to see her. (Maybe I could pick-up the thread from there…) Hesitantly, I went to her house and rang the bell. A young lady opened the door; there she was – Mijntje; somehow I didn't believe she was real. She invited me in, and judging from the pictures on the wall, she was now married. We talked for awhile about old times, and suddenly I felt the urge to leave and so I did. It made no sense to cling to something that wasn't there anymore. I had to find someone else to help me help back into 'normal life'.

When I returned to the factory housing, there was a note for me saying that an uncle of mine had come to visit me and that he would return the next day. The following day, he came back. He was my mother's youngest brother who had survived the war with his wife and son by going 'underground' during the last stages of the war. They were living in Hilversum now; a town located nearly sixty miles from Amsterdam. And when my uncle invited me to come and stay with them – I accepted readily. I picked up my belongings and left the old diamond factory to move to Hilversum the following day.

My uncle confirmed the deportation of my parents. On the other hand my sister's deportation was somewhat of a mystery to me. It seemed that she had moved in with my uncle and his family at the time she had discovered that my parents had disappeared. But they never explained to my satisfaction how it was possible for them to have survived the war unscathed while my sister had been deported. My uncle told me that apparently she had volunteered to go when her boyfriend was picked up; a story which I accepted but did not quite believe. She survived the war but died a couple days after the Liberation along with my mother who had been sent to the same camp in Sweden to await their transfer home to Holland. She and my mother hadn't been able to withstand the onslaught of typhoid and succumbed to it.

After a short while at my uncle's place I realized that staying in Hilversum was not the answer. In order to get back into circulation I could not doze off in a little town but I had to go back to the big city. Consequently, I moved back to Amsterdam. By accident I discovered that my best friend Gerrie who had disappeared in the early days of the war was still alive and well. His family had also gone underground. And even though they had lived in very difficult conditions during that time, they had survived. They offered to take me in and helped me to start a new life.

I went back to Kattenburg and asked them if they could give me my old job back – they promptly put me in the same department where I used to work before I was taken away to Germany. The problem was that after working on the outside for so long, it was hard for me to adjust to being confined between four walls. And it occurred to me that when I looked around me I saw people sitting *where they didn't belong*. Everyone reminded me of other men and women who would never come back. All of the people that had been picked up on that terrible night three years earlier had been exterminated except for the three of us that had returned. I became evident that as long as I stayed at Kattenburg, the ghosts of all those people with whom I used to work would haunt me.

One night, when I was leaving the factory, I was surprised to see Anny at the door waiting for me. Word had reached her – she had been told that I survived and she came to see if she could do anything to help me. It was a surprise and heartwarming to know that the girl I was so eager to save from prostitution was there wanting to help me. She held a baby in her arms which was born during the years I had been away. She once told me that she couldn't have children – and here was the living proof that doctors could make mistakes too. She had been married but the marriage ended in a divorce within a year. So, she was alone again and wanting to know if we could rekindle our former relationship. She said she was 'out of the business' and asked if I could come and visit her, the following Saturday. On the day we discussed everything we could think of – including marriage. I considered that this would be a big step for me, but a step in the right direction – starting a new life with a ready-made family. I was all ears. When it seemed that everything was settled, her mother was called and informed of our plans. Suddenly a big obstacle was put in the way of our union. Everything was going to be called off unless I converted to the Catholic faith. It was all over in a moment – Goodbye Anny. I believed that as long as you believed in God, it did not matter what religion you followed – wrong again! And another illusion smashed to pieces.

I was determined to leave Kattenburg. I applied at another factory and was hired almost immediately. Slowly, but surely, I started to fit into the civilian life again.

In order not to lose contact with the only uncle I had left, I made it a habit to seeing him once in a while. On one such occasion, we decided to make an effort and try to regain possession of the banana plant to put it back in the hands of our family. We had high hopes. My uncle took upon himself to do all of the necessary leg work and I didn't mind. I was sure he would be up to the task since he had as much interest in the plant as I did and he knew all of the people involved. Actually all he needed from me was some financial support to pay for all of the costs attached to the repossessing of the plant. But if the deal came through we would have an income that would help us live comfortably and by the same token we would be able to regain some of the glory that once belonged to our family.

Every time he got back from his many meetings with the government agencies, the picture looked brighter. But, after three years we were still kept in suspense. Although the picture still looked bright – we couldn't see any tangible results on the horizon. Then I remembered that my father and I had buried my grandmother's family jewels in the old house. Thus, one day I paid a visit to the people who lived there now. I asked them to allow me to dig up the loot. They granted me permission to do so and in no time at all I found the place where our little treasure was hidden – they were as curious as I was to see it. I lifted the floorboard in the hallway and to everyone dismay there was nothing there. I was dumfounded. Later I found out that my grandmother, who was a very suspicious lady, had called on my uncle and had asked him to dig up the jewelry box and hide it someplace else. The only uncle who could have done it was the very same uncle with whom I was working to regain possession of the plant. When I confronted him with the evidence, he denied having any part in this scheme... Yet he was the only person who knew where the gems were hidden. At long last he confessed to have taken the jewels and used them to save his and his family lives. I would have had no objections at all in him doing that if it hadn't been for the fact that he lied to me in the first place. And I became more and more suspicious of his dealings during the war – and from that point in time, for me the case was closed. I had never been rich, so what difference did it make? But my hope was still to regain control of the banana plant.

A few months later I learned that my uncle finally got the plant back into family hands – his son is running it today. Good luck to him...

Meanwhile my social life was getting back *to normal*... My grandfather's soccer club didn't exist anymore and since not many people returned from the war there was no way to justify rebuilding it. So, if it wasn't this club, I would join another – and that's what I did with the help of a friend. Soccer had been, and would be, a very important part of my life.

I also met a girl whom I liked very much. She introduced me to her family and I was immediately 'adopted'. This was very important to me; I needed people around me so not to fall into depression or at the grip of loneliness – and this family provided that for me. They were a very close-knitted family and it made me feel very comfortable.

As for the relationship itself however, it failed miserably. I could not adjust to a life of fun and pleasure anymore. Whenever we went to a party, there would always be a low point in the evening when I would start thinking of the many people I had lost in my young life and so many of them being members of my family; that sure enough I ended up depressed and morose. I think this is something not many people could understand. Apart from my own misgivings about my behavior, I was sure she had a relationship with someone else. My suspicions were confirmed during a party we attended. Even though she knew I could not dance, she convinced me to go to a party where she said there would be a show besides the dancing, and I could enjoy myself as well. It turned out that it was a night of dancing and drinking – and no show... I have never felt so lonesome in my life, not only for the fact that I had to sit out every dance but seeing all of those people having fun and being conned by my own girlfriend made me feel even worse. At around eleven that night, Kitty became very obnoxious and began to tease me. It was apparent that she had too much to drink and had no control over what she was doing or saying. And, when she started humiliating me in front of 'the other guy', I had had enough – she had gone too far this time; I grabbed her hand and pulled her towards me. I asked her to go home with me immediately… The guy *ordered* me to let go of her hand. This was all he had to say… He offered me the perfect opportunity to release my anger and frustration and planting a few fists into his jaw. The short fight ended in my winning the round and losing my girl. I had won the fight and lost my rage in the space of a few minutes.

It was back to square one… However, one night I went to the movie theater with Gerrie and more than a movie I saw an usherette by the name of Elizabeth… She really opened the door of renewed hope; I felt alive again.

The rest is a story I'd like to tell and which will be the subject of our next book –

I am (not) a survivor
I am a striver

ABOUT THE AUTHOR

Roxane is a professional editor/writer and has been so for the past twenty years. She has been educated in the art of writing in both English and French since the age of fourteen. She has participated in the writing of many books and in the editing of many more manuscripts. From highly technical subjects to romances, religious discourses and stories of all kinds, she has had the privilege of encountering several styles, genres and talents whilst meeting many writers and authors who have all taught her something, she says. Yet, when it comes to this story, Roxane gives the reader a further insight into her past: "As for me, I am only a writer who saw in Lou Van Coevorden the opportunity to tell the story of some of my family – the ones who didn't make it; those whom I will never meet, those who have disappeared because they were of another race."

"I wish for this book to be an inspiration for future generations and a guiding thought for those who would be led by leaders thirsty for power and lusting for the sadistic enthroning of their imaginary strength."

Printed in the United States
25809LVS00001B/7-57